Praise from others for *the feel-good heat: Pioneers in Corn and Biomass Energy—*

Since the first settlers crossed the Mississippi River and began to call Iowa home, the pioneering spirit has been an integral part of being an Iowan. It is this pioneering spirit that has propelled Iowa into the forefront of the bio-energy revolution. Innovation and hard work have resulted in hundreds of towns and cities in this great state cultivating strong economies and close-knit communities.

Individuals can also be bio-energy pioneers. One person or family can make a difference by installing corn burning stoves and other devices to heat their homes. That small change will reduce America's dependence on fossil fuels and make our state and nation more energy secure. I want to congratulate Ed Williams and Sheila Samuelson for creating *The Feel Good Heat* and demonstrating the ease and comfort that can be achieved by using biomass to heat their homes. This book is an invaluable resource for any person that has ever wondered what they can do to improve their state, nation, and world.

—Lt. Governor Patty Judge, State of Iowa

If you're like me, you probably feel pretty powerless when it comes to dealing with the twin global problems (and catastrophes in the making) of oil addiction and environmental degradation. But you and I can act at the individual and community levels, starting by reading *The Feel-Good Heat*. Sheila Samuelson has written an accessible overview of energy alternatives, coupled with real-world examples of how individuals have converted their homes and businesses from petroleum-based to biomass heating. Reduce your household energy expenditures by purchasing the book for yourself, and invest in our world's future by sending another to your representative in Washington.

—Joe Tye, author, *The Farmer: A Story of West Central & Never Fear, Never Quit*

While the rest of us try to figure out how to harness biomass energy for economical power and transportation fuels, Ed Williams and other corn stove pioneers are demonstrating that consumers can already make a difference by heating their homes and businesses with biomass. Sheila Samuelson documents the story of corn stoves in her book *The Feel Good Heat*, which includes descriptions of bioenergy and corn stove technology as well as extensive interviews with "burners" and industry experts. Any one considering the purchase of a corn stove or simply wanting to understand this new business will be interested in reading *The Feel Good Heat*.

—Robert C. Brown, Iowa State University, Professor, Department of Agricultural and Biosystems Engineering, Director, Office of Biorenewables Programs

Climate change is caused by a lot of things, and it will take a lot of people to fix it. The "pioneers" featured in *The Feel Good Heat* are demonstrating that individuals and families can reduce their carbon emissions by adopting alternative energy technologies right in their own homes and businesses. This well written book by Sheila Samuelson may very well have the power to convince others to do the same.

    —Jill Euken ISU Extension/CIRAS (Center for Industrial Research And Service), Industrial Specialist, Biobased Products

The creation of a biobased economy will take a broadbased and concerted effort to find as many ways as we can to utilize renewable crops and crop residues. Creation of a new economy will undoubtedly be an evolution. *The Feel Good Heat* is a good example of simple, direct, first steps that can be taken by consumers to support the biobased movement.

    —Brent Erickson, Executive vice president in charge of the Industrial and Environmental Section at the Biotechnology Industry Organization, Washington, DC

As the editor of an environmental-design magazine, I know there's no better way to demonstrate the benefits of a unique technology than through testimonials. *The Feel Good Heat* provides the business and environmental case for corn stoves through biomass experts and stove owners—their greatest champions. As energy prices increase, it's time we all look to renewable energy sources we can "feel good" about!

    —Christina Koch, editor, *eco-structure* magazine

In the emerging sustainable world one can anticipate, demonstrate, or participate. Century Farm Harvest Heat owner Ed Williams is accomplishing all three. The choice and challenge to the reader is to dive into biomass on a personal level—anticipate, demonstrate and participate in making a difference. Williams shares a lifetime of knowledge in a truthful and succinct manner. Will you join?

    —Wendy Gady, Emissary, Renewable On Parade

Having worked for the Iowa City Public School District over 40 years, both in the classroom and in the Media Center, I have learned that you never fail to learn something if you read. After hearing dire predictions of global-warming, the shortage of energy and fuel, it is refreshing to read a book that looks to a solution to a problem. The book was very informative and knowledgeable. I found myself learning a lot from the testimonials of people that have experimented and found it successful.

  Just think, we would be helping the environment and our pocketbooks!

    —Sandy Slothower, retired, Iowa City School District

the feel-good heat

Pioneers Of Corn and Biomass Energy

Sheila Samuelson

with Ed Williams of
Century Farm Harvest Heat

The Ice Cube Press
North Liberty, Iowa USA

the feel-good heat:
Pioneers Of Corn and Biomass Energy

Copyright © 2007 Sheila Samuelson, editor & Ed Williams
Century Farm Harvest Heat

Isbn 9781888160291 (1-888160-29-2)

Library of Congress Control Number: 2006939897

Ice Cube Press (est. 1993)
205 North Front Street
North Liberty, Iowa 52317-9302
www.icecubepress.com

Manufactured in the United States of America on recycled paper.

The paper used in this publication meets the minimum requirements of the American National Standard for Information Sciences—Permanence of Paper for Printed Library Materials, ANSI Z39.48-1992

George Washington Carver photo on page 3 is from the Library of Congress, public domain research division, <http://www.loc.gov/rr/print/list/235_poc.html>.

Disclaimer: unless specified, the views in this book on using corn or pellet stoves are those of the individuals and do not constitute an endorsement of any particular corn or pellet stove, manufacturer, or reseller. Nor are these individuals experts at the operation, or installation of corn/pellet stoves. One should always follow the manufacturers' recommendations for proper installation and operation. Stove performance is based upon brand, installation, operation, care and other factors including, but not limited to, corn quality, weather and proper maintenance.

This book is dedicated to the memory and work of George Washington Carver (c.1864-1943), an important leader, scholar, inventor, visionary, philosopher, artist, botanist and agricultural researcher. He attended Simpson College in Indianola, Iowa and later, was the first African-American student and faculty member at Iowa State University.

"I believe that the great Creator has put ores and oil on this earth to give us a breathing spell. As we exhaust them, we must be prepared to fall back on our farms, which is God's true storehouse and can never be exhausted. We can learn to synthesize material for every human need from things that grow."
—George Washington Carver, US horticulturist

This book was only possible with the contributions of the following people and their dedication to biomass as a clean, renewable source of energy. Thank you to: Ed Williams, Steve Semken and Ice Cube Press, Joe Sharpnack, Michelle Provorse, Mary and Dominic Audia, Mark Hartstack, Connie Prusha and Prusha Napa Auto, Willard Huedepohl, Father Anthony Good, Mary and Kevin Sommerville, Albert Dose, Carolyn Zaiser, Doug Yansky and Doug Yansky Auto, Alisa and Josh Meggitt, Dan Black, Cindy Mays and Iowa State Bank & Trust, Jerry and Pam Ausman, Dennis Doderer, Steve and Sonja Moss, Gary Scott, Jim Shepherd, Zac and Elesa Wedemeyer, David Zollo, Jim Heineman and The Fancy Street Clock & Light Co., Inc., Ken Kemper and Twisted Pair Post, Darren and Beck West, Bob and Karen Dose, Glen and Maggie Mowery, Kathrin Schmidt, Glen and Ginger Hanson, Dave Jackson, Michael Ott, Jay Wheeler, Bill Bliss, Dennis Buffington, Gayla D Paul, Becky and Darin West, Robert Walker, Lee Strait, John Wagor, Allan Cagnoli, Jim Crutcher, Don Kaiser, Kristina Koch, Margaret Wieting, Tammy Richardson and Richard Fox and Troy Price.

the feel-good heat

Table of Contents

Introduction
Ed Williams, Century Farm Harvest Heat

We've referred to those included in this book as pioneers, but to find the earliest risk takers we should really go back twenty years. After all, it was garage tinkerers and shade tree mechanics who fiddled and finagled with motors, blowers, augers and plates of steel in search of just a little energy independence before "alternative/renewable/biomass/biofuel/sustainable" was COOL!

I believe the image of pioneers striking out in a wagon train for unsettled lands is an apt one regarding biomass energy. No one included in the following pages thinks of themselves as enduring anything like the hardships experienced by the original settlers, but each has required a certain out-of-the-box, adventurous mindset to set off for this transformation into a new era of energy. Century Farm Harvest Heat has placed more than 300 stoves into homes during the past five years. The community has expanded as the wagon train traveled onward. Patience, involvement, vision…all seem to be necessary qualities to make this journey bearable. We're all learning, sharing and helping each other.

I still remember watching my first SnowFlame corn stove come to life in 2002 and being fascinated with the whole process—how the corn kernels dropped into the glowing embers, became charred and blackened right before a small whiff of smoke would arise and then watching as the kernels burst into tiny blue, then yellow flames—seemed somewhat miraculous. As the fan kicked in and the warmth from the stove flowed into my face, I knew, right then, this technology was only at its infancy. As *Nature* magazine stated in the December, 2006, issue: "Biomass energy is an idea whose time has returned."

Naysayers have abounded. "You're burning food… The energy used to grow the corn is more than what's created… It sounds like a lot of work… Corn's gonna get expensive." We've heard it all. Solar, wind, geothermal, hydrogen are all wonderful alternatives which play an important role in energy independence. But these funky lil' corn and pellet stoves are right here, right now, with the fastest economic return on investment by far.

I've often wondered who coined the term "Natural" gas. This label was truly a marketing coup! Yes the gas comes from within the earth, but so does "natural" oil. Both start out crude and must be processed by very unnatural means then transported thousands of miles to be combusted and made useful. Biomass, be it corn, pecan hulls, olive pits, cotton seed ... is a regional fuel. The beauty of a BioEconomy is that one person's waste stream becomes another person's starting point. As today's corn prices approach $150/ton, we're looking at $20/ton ethanol by-products for BTU content and burn suitability.

But for those you'll read about in the following pages, it's not all about cost per unit, economic Bottom Line or return on investment. In a recent discussion with a 3rd year Harvest Heat stove owner, who is an engineer at Rockwell Collins in Cedar Rapids, I was pointing out the inevitable ebb and flow of corn prices versus energy costs. He responded with, "Ed, they could pay me to burn their damn gas, and I wouldn't do it anymore!" Extreme? Yes, but fairly typical of the pioneer can-do attitude you'll read about in this book.

Once considered a fad, corn burning/biomass technology is now a global phenomenon. A year ago, I was stunned when an Italian engineering firm contacted me through our web site searching for "corn burning technology to diffuse throughout Europe." At that time, with demand outstripping supply, I had to inform them that, "Shoot, there's not enough corn burning technology to diffuse throughout Iowa!" Today,

IOWA AND PIONEERS. Biomass isn't the first time we've encountered the need and will for the pioneer spirit. Being a pioneer is as much a frame of mind as it is using biomass for energy. A classic example of this is Century Farm Harvest Heat's owner Ed Williams', great-great-grandmother, Mrs. Phebe Davis Williams (1808-1885). Who, from her obituary, "was one of the oldest citizens of Johnson County [Iowa], settling here when these finely improved farms were wild prairie. It was interesting to hear her relate her experiences of pioneer life. She knew its privations and trials, and of these she had her full share."

as demand and supply become balanced, manufacturers around the globe are adding corn burning technology to their line up as they experiment, create and try to develop the next wave in this exciting era of renewable energy.

I heard a futurist three years ago at my first BIO conference implore those attending to, "Work together to expand the bioeconomy and get back to competition later." The oil and gas industries have had decades to build their infrastructure and solidify their power, while those in the alternative energy arena have remained fractured and disjointed. The technologies continue to improve in *all* alternative energies, and it will take *all* of them to displace any significant segment of our traditional energy sources.

In any emerging trend, consumer acceptance and demand play a critical role. The "early innovators" you'll read about in the following pages have been inspiring. They've made the leap into an emerging industry and have provided valuable input to dealers and manufacturers as new software, hardware, and business systems have evolved.

The "Triple Bottom Line" model, where economic, environmental and societal sustainability *all* contribute to the success of a business is a concept whose time has arrived. Century Farm Harvest Heat has been guided by this concept during our first five years. As we move forward we'd like to bring together manufacturers, corporate sponsors and fuel producers (farmers and pellet producers) to place heaters in churches, business and non-profit facilities creating the proverbial win/win.

As you read the stories that follow, we hope you begin to understand and consider not if, but when you'll be ready to join this growing community. On the one hand, you'll see a diverse group with varied reasons for getting on board: economic return, environmental sustainability, stickin' it to the man, or just plain "feelin' good while feelin' warm". But, on the other hand, they all possess the vision, patience, and willingness to be truly involved in this new frontier.

We thank you for coming this far in your own willingness to explore. Enjoy!

Energy and the Environment

Non-renewable Energy

The difference between renewable and non-renewable energy is its source, and the rate at which that source is replenished. Over hundreds of millions of years, coal, oil and natural gas would be considered renewable energies, so long as conditions were conducive to their production. This long time scale is not effective in human terms, and these

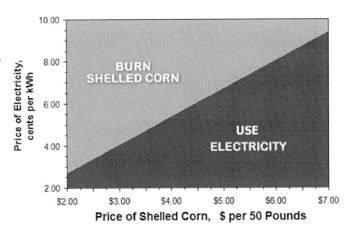

resources are considered non-renewable fossil fuels. As fossil fuels are consumed, reserves are depleted, without the possibility of becoming abundant again for many millions of years.

Coal, oil and natural gas are the carbon remains of plants and animals from geologic ages past, and their combustion releases carbon, long stored beneath the surface of the earth, into the atmosphere as carbon dioxide (CO_2). Highly combustible, and the primary source of power for much of the world throughout the 20th century, fossil fuels bring with them consequences that environmental scientists began detecting in the 1970s. CO_2 and other greenhouse gases that occur naturally in our atmosphere trap radiant heat emitted from the surface of our planet, making Earth a warm, habitable place for life to exist. Though large on a human scale, the atmosphere is but a thin shell surrounding the Earth, and even small changes in its composition affect how it functions and how much heat it retains or allows to pass. The more heat it allows to pass, the cooler the Earth's climate, and vice versa.

Climate Change

The vast majority of scientists today agree that humans have dramatically increased the amount of carbon in the atmosphere, fueling global climate change. Between the years 1750 and 2003 the concentration of CO_2 in the Earth's atmosphere has increased 32% from 280 to 376 parts per million, largely due to the widespread combustion of fossil fuels and changes in land use[1]. Approximately 60% of that increase has taken place since 1959. During this time, the average global temperature has risen by 0.6° C, (1.08° F) a relatively large and alarming jump[2]. The resulting climate change has already led to many documented warning signs such as glacial melting, increased intensity and frequency of extreme weather events—the number of category 4 and 5 hurricanes has almost doubled in the last 30 years[3]—and shifting habitat ranges of plants, animals and insects. At least 279 species of plants and animals are responding to global warming by moving closer to the poles[4]. These warning signs, and others such as widespread coral bleaching, early arrival of spring, increased droughts and wildfires, heavy precipitation and flooding, sea-level rise and coastal flooding, are occurring now at rates never experienced in human history[5].

Ecosystem Degradation

Degradation and unsustainable use of ecosystem services has been prevalent in the past 50 years. Food, fiber, fuel, fresh water, genetic resources, biochemicals, natural medicines, climate regulation, air and water quality regulation, waste treatment, erosion control, and aesthetic enjoyment are all provided free by nature, but the abundance and quality of these products and services is diminishing.

The worldwide mining and consumption of natural resources and accumulation of waste, toxic and otherwise, has gone largely unchecked—and often under-regulated. Fueled largely by widespread consumption and a growing demand for fossil fuels in industrialized countries, mining of fossil fuels involves extracting materials from within the earth by cutting deep trenches, drilling, or removing surface layers of earth, which is more often than not, catastrophic to the balance of the ecosystem. As land is torn up, excavated, and exposed like an open wound on the surface of the Earth, habitats are destroyed and erosion quickly washes away soil, clay, rocks and plant and animal life, no longer held intact by a matrix of topsoil. Massive erosion events are a pollutant to natural waters, compromising the ability of streams and wetlands to be hospitable places for life by lowering oxygen levels, overloading nutrients and minerals, prohibiting the passage of light, etc. Because mining and exploration of fossil fuels widely takes place in wild and rural areas, the impact on ecosystems is often significant.

The financial impact of the loss of services provided by the ecosystem can be incredibly hard to measure in terms of dollars, but it is clear that degradation of ecosystem services represents the loss of a capital asset. The long-term value of managing ecosystems more efficiently is often higher than the associated value of intensive, short-term uses. In fact, damage to the ecosystem can be linked to substantial long term economic and public health costs[6].

In nature, ecosystem changes generally occur in a predictable, gradual and incremental fashion and the effects of non-linear changes are hard to predict and manage. Established, yet incomplete evidence demonstrates that unsustainable ecosystem use increases the likelihood of abrupt and irreversible future ecosystem changes with important consequences to human well-being[7]. Known consequences include potentially catastrophic events such as disease emergence, eutrophication and hypoxia of fresh water and coastal areas (killing most marine life), spread of invasive species and extinction, and regional climate change[8].

Together, the effects of climate-changing atmospheric CO_2 and widespread ecosystem degradation present a major challenge both for the natural world and society. Both are due in part to the demand, acquisition and use of non-renewable fuels.

Oil

Crude oil consists of plant and animal remains from hundreds of millions of years ago which, covered by layers of sediment and under extreme pressure, anaerobic conditions and high temperature, have become an organic chemical compound of liquid carbon and hydrogen (hydrocarbons). Oil refineries break these hydrocarbons down into gasoline, diesel fuel and heating oil, jet fuel, heavy fuel oil, liquefied petroleum gas

(LPG) and other products. World oil usage in 2005 increased 1.3% from 2004 to 83.3 million barrels per day, of which 20 million barrels were consumed daily in the US[9].

Natural Gas

Composed mainly of methane (CH_4), natural gas is a fossil fuel found in gaseous form. Natural gas, a greenhouse gas, is produced by the same geological process as oil and can be found in natural gas and oil fields and in coal beds. Methane is the lightest and the smallest of the hydrocarbons and, being lighter than

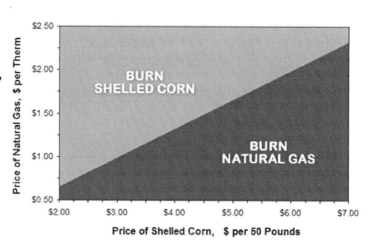

air, easily disperses into the atmosphere. Natural gas is used to turn turbines for power generators, in hydrogen production, in the production of fertilizers, and the manufacture of many other products, such as fabrics, steel, paint and plastics.

Coal

Coal formation also takes place over millions of years, as plant remains that have become buried under swamps are deprived of oxygen, compacted, hardened, chemically altered and metamorphosed. Coal is a solid fuel used primarily for heat production through combustion within a boiler. Electricity production with steam produced from this heat accounts for 75% of world coal consumption. Coal is the leading source of fuel for electricity production, worldwide, though modern coal-fired power plants average only 33% efficiency in converting energy into electricity.

Renewable Energy

Increasing global population and industrialization indicates that both ecosystem degradation and climate change could occur much more rapidly and grow significantly worse during the first half of the 21st century. The growing demands for some ecosystem services, however, may be eased by modern technological response, providing increased energy efficiency, reduced greenhouse gas emissions, and technologies to increase crop yields without harmful impacts related to water, nutrient and pesticide use.

Renewable energies are so named because their sources are derived from an inexhaustible supply, such as the sun, wind, biomass, ocean tides, and flowing water (which may at times be exhaustible). These sources can largely be harnessed indefinitely without depletion of their supplies, which are constantly being replenished on a time scale that is useful in human terms. Renewable sources of energy are often locally based, providing employment and property tax revenue and eliminating the need to ship or pipe fuels from far away. Development of renewables will diversify the energy portfolios of regional economies, making them less vulnerable to the volatile trends of fossil fuel prices. Other merits of renewable energy production include substantial reduction (and sometimes elimination) of CO_2 and other pollutants when used in place of fossil fuels, and in many cases, little or no ecosystem degradation.

That is not to say, however, that there are not environmental concerns, real and perceived, related to renewable energy production, or that renewable energy will be a viable solution in every case. Conscious engineering and design, advances in renewable energy technology, and public awareness will alleviate some of these challenges, which are discussed in more detail below.

The use of renewable energy sources is gradually becoming more prevalent. Renewable energy is generally used to generate electricity and heat buildings, with very little used for transportation. The last 33 years have seen a 2.3% average annual growth of renewable supply, compared to a 2.1% growth of the total primary energy supply. As of 2003, renewables constituted 13.3% of the world's total primary energy supply. Broken down further, biomass and combustible waste products made up 10.6% of the world's power. Hydropower accounted for 2.2% of world power while the combination of wind, solar, wave and geothermal accounted for less than one half a percent[10].

Solar Energy

Directly or indirectly, the source of most energy available on Earth comes from the sun. Heat and light from the sun provide an abundant source of energy that can be harnessed in many ways. These include passive lighting and heating of homes and non-residential buildings, generating hot water, solar cooling, converting sunlight directly into electricity with photovoltaics (PV), and concentrating sunlight to heat water for electricity generation in power plants. Solar energy is a domestically produced source of power that is generally reliable.

Passive solar heating is a design principle which takes advantage of the heat and light on a building's south facing side (in the Northern Hemisphere), by allowing light to pass through windows and heat to be stored in floor and wall materials with a high thermal mass, or ability to retain heat. In this way, heat stored during the day is slowly released throughout the night. Passive solar lighting is the brightening of interior spaces using strategically placed windows. The greatest benefit of passive solar design is its efficient, conscious use of the sun as a free, abundant source of both heat and light. Drawbacks to passive solar could include overheating during summer months. There are design features, however, that minimize sunlight and heat during the summer months and maximize it during the winter.

Photovoltaics, or solar cells, directly convert light (photons) to electricity (voltage) as the absorption of sunlight allows electron flow. PV cell arrays can be mounted at a fixed angle toward the sun, as with solar shingles, or track the sun throughout the day. Concentrating collectors use a curved lens to focus the sunlight onto the cell in an attempt to minimize PV material and maximize the use of solar energy, but require sophisticated tracking devices. While the efficiency of PVs is improving, only about 15% of sunlight striking the cell generates electricity, because only sunlight of certain wavelengths will work efficiently to create energy, and much of it is reflected or absorbed by the material that makes up the cell[11].

Solar hot water systems are made up of two parts, a collector and a storage tank. The collector is a thin, dark colored box that faces the sun and absorbs heat, which it transfers to the fluid flowing through small tubes running through the box. The tubes are attached to a storage tank, which holds the water.

Geothermal Energy

Geo (Earth) thermal (heat) energy is heat from the Earth that is captured from the hot water, steam, hot rock, and someday perhaps magma, beneath the surface of the Earth. Circulating air pumped through shallow wells takes advantage of the relatively constant temperature of about 50-60° F (10-16° C) maintained just below Earth's surface to heat and cool buildings. In colder climates, the heat pump generally provides the majority of the heat, but works in tandem with another source to provide sufficient warmth. Hot water and steam reservoirs in the Western United States are tapped by drilling deep into the earth, and the energy is used for district heating, melting snow on sidewalks and streets, or other applications. Wells (a mile or more deep) can tap into even hotter water and steam that can be used to turn electricity-generating turbines.

Merits of geothermal energy include the abundance of this enormous and underused source of heat and power; the cleanliness of the energy, which requires almost no fossil fuels to produce, releasing very few, if any nitrous oxide or sulfur-bearing gases; the reliability of this constant, year-round heat source; and the fact that geothermal energy is domestic, aiding in the energy independence of local economies. The high initial investment of geothermal plants and heat pumps is balanced by lower operation and maintenance costs.

Wind Power

Wind is an indirect form of solar energy. Caused by uneven heating of the Earth's atmosphere, winds are masses of air moving towards equilibrium from high- to low-pressure areas. A wind turbine converts the kinetic energy in winds into mechanical power, which can then be converted into electricity. Small wind turbines can be grid-connected, in which the local utility makes up for energy demand the turbine cannot meet, and pays the owner for excess energy that the turbine produces, called net-metering. Stand-alone small wind systems can be ideal for remote locations without access to utility lines.

Wind is a clean, renewable, local and plentiful source of energy. No air pollutants or atmospheric emissions are produced while generating power from wind, and the US Department of Energy reports that just 6% of the contiguous United States land area has the potential to supply more than 1.5 times the current electricity consumption in the US. Even large turbines require only a fraction of an acre, allowing rural areas to continue crop production. The affordability of wind power, in many cases 4 to 6 cents per kilowatt-hour, makes it one of the most cost-effective renewable energy technologies today.

Even with all the benefits listed above, wind power is not suited for many situations. Abundant wind is often located far from cities, where it is most needed, and windy periods do not always coincide with energy demand. Though wind energy is affordable per kilowatt-hour, the initial investment of wind technology can be a barrier. Another hindrance to wind power has been public perception: some consider turbines unsightly, while others fear noise pollution and bird fatalities, which were both once challenges.

Hydropower

The hydrologic cycle constantly moves water in a pattern of evaporation and precipitation, driven by the sun. The energy of this cycle, and specifically large quantities of moving water, can be harnessed to turn turbines to produce electricity or for mechanical tasks. In this way, water is a fuel that is not consumed in the process of producing hydropower, making it a renewable energy.

Because the movement of water is fueled by the sun, creation of hydropower is not associated with release of air pollutants. In addition to cleanliness, hydropower is abundant and can be used as needed by controlling flow of water through turbines.

Despite the benefits, there are a number of serious environmental caveats associated with using water to create electricity. Downstream water flow and quality can be impacted to the point that habitats are adversely affected. Dams present a challenge to fish populations migrating to spawning grounds or the ocean, if devices to allow passage of fish are not in place. Entire habitats are lost by creation of reservoirs, displacing plant, animal and sometimes human life.

Nuclear

Twenty percent of electricity in the US is derived from nuclear fission, which harnesses the energy from the nuclei of processed Uranium mined from the ground. Nuclear power does not produce greenhouse gases and is renewable to the extent that Uranium is renewable. The nuclear industry grew rapidly in the 1970s and 1980s, but cost overruns in maintaining nuclear power plants, the higher price of nuclear power and catastrophic accidents have cooled industry growth in recent years. Uranium is toxic and radioactive in all isotopes and compounds, and exposure by ingestion or inhalation of fine dust produced by mining can lead to kidney damage and pulmonary diseases.

Biomass...

See next chapter!

What is Biomass?

Biomass is plant matter or plant-derived material, rich with the sun's energy that has been captured by photosynthesis. (An even broader definition includes all organic non-fossil material, i.e. all biological organisms and their metabolic by-products.) For our purposes, the term biomass is often used to refer to plant material used specifically for heat and power production. Biomass comes in many forms, and includes starchy grains or oily seeds, the leaves and stems of soft-bodied plants, wood, and many other feedstocks. Each region will have different forms of available biomass depending on the local agricultural and industries present. A lumber community generates wood scraps and sawdust, while a rural agricultural community may harvest the cornstalk residue. Both could be considered waste, or they could be recognized as value-added byproducts full of energy that can be utilized for local heat and power generation.

Biomass is a localized, domestic energy supply—as an already-existing industry by-product or a crop that can be grown on the time scale of days or months—as opposed to fossil fuels, which take millions of years to form and the source of which is very rarely local, but must be shipped across continents or halfway around the world. This gives biomass an economic advantage, as it injects and retains money in local communities; and a security advantage, adding to energy independence, making the country less dependent on the often-unstable regimes that control much of the world's oil.

Finally, the use of biomass has clear environmental advantages over fossil fuel use. Because bio-based fuels are localized, less energy is consumed in delivery to the customer. For example, heating homes with natural gas requires the gas, once pumped from underground reserves and highly processed, be shipped and piped long distances to the end user. Heating a home with corn or a biomass pellet, requires fuel transport only from the local farm or pelleting plant directly to a neighborhood store, or delivery to your home. (Of course the energy used to produce crops and pellets must be accounted for in the overall energy equation, but increasingly efficient farming techniques and pelleting processes continue to make biomass products efficient alternatives.) While burning fossil fuels contributes significant amounts of CO_2 into the atmosphere, the combustion of biomass products releases an equivalent amount of CO_2 to that which was absorbed during the growth of the plant matter, making it a carbon-neutral process: burning biomass does not contribute to the amount of CO_2 in the atmosphere.

Biomass is a rapidly growing piece of the US energy portfolio, and recognition of its value and ability to provide economic, reliable alternative energy is on the rise. The U.S. Department of Energy reports that in 2003, biomass was the leading source of renewable energy in the United States, accounting for 4% of total energy used, and 47% of all renewable energy.

Energy in plant matter

Three billion years ago, a crude precursor of modern photosynthesis first stored solar energy into chemical bonds. The oxygen-releasing photosynthetic process of today became important two billion years ago, when Earth's inhabitants were cyanobacteria and their still mostly single-celled prokaryotic neighbors. More recently, eukaryotic cells developed, including photosynthetic plant species, incorporating cellular machinery called chlorophyll to perform the energy conversion and give plants their characteristic green color.

During the photosynthetic process, light energy captured by chlorophyll is combined with CO_2 from the air, and water from the ground in a series of photosynthetic reactions (the light-dependent and light-independent reactions and the Calvin cycle), producing the by-product oxygen, and the energy-containing sugar molecule, glucose.

Plants, as carbon-based life forms, utilize carbon which is readily available in the biosphere and atmosphere for growth and photosynthesis. This carbon is part of the natural carbon cycle, and is released back into the atmosphere during respiration (the opposite action of photosynthesis), plant decay, or during combustion (which is the opposite of plant growth). Combusting fossil fuels, however, does introduce carbon (CO_2), that has been stored for so long that the carbon is no longer considered part of the cycle, thus, the use of fossil fuels, in opposition to the use of biomass as fuel, does create a net carbon gain in the atmosphere.

The photosynthesis equation:

$$6CO_2 + 12H_2O + \text{light energy} \rightarrow C_6H_{12}O_6 + 6O_2 + 6H_2O$$

Glucose, a carbohydrate and a six carbon simple sugar, stores the energy to drive cell functions and in its various forms, is the source of energy in biomass. From simple sugars to complex polymers, the forms of sugar found in biomass represent a range of possibilities for energy production, from simple combustion to ethanol production.

Uses for Biomass

Transportation

Biomass is a fully renewable feedstock for power and heat production. Though it is not possible for biomass to replace 100% of the energy consumed today, when coupled with fuel conservation methods and increasingly efficient biorefineries, biomass-derived energy will significantly reduce reliance on fossil fuels.

The US consumes nearly 21 million barrels of petroleum daily—that's about 3 gallons per person per day. According to the U.S. Energy Information Administration (EIA), transportation accounts for a stunning 69% of our oil consumption. Biomass alternatives to oil and petroleum-based transportation fuels are already a reality, and are being used around the globe. In fact, the EIA predicts a substantial increase in biofuels as a result of higher projected prices for traditional fuels, and the Energy Policy Act, 2005 Federal legislation, introducing support for alternative fuels.

Bioethanol, also known as simply ethanol, is a clean-burning alcohol produced from crops such as corn or sugarcane, and combined in varying proportions with traditional fossil fuel. A mixture of 10% ethanol and 90% unleaded gasoline, known as E10, is safe for use in any gasoline vehicle in the US. The American Coalition for Ethanol reports that in 2004, about one-third of America's gasoline was blended with ethanol, most as E10. E85 (85% ethanol, 15% gasoline) is safe for use in the more than four million Flex Fuel Vehicles, which can run on straight gasoline or any ethanol blend up to 85%.

Ethanol production alone is growing from a niche to a nationwide market. There are nearly 200 ethanol production facilities in operation or construction in the US, and half of which are farmer-owned cooperatives. Between 1997 and 2005 production has more than tripled, jumping from 1.3 billion gallons to over 4 billion gallons per year. By the year 2030, the EIA expects an annual production of 14.6 billion gallons, which will account for 8% of gasoline consumption by volume.

Historically, there has been debate about the energy efficiency of ethanol, but the US Department of Energy (DOE) life-cycle reports show that production of ethanol is energy efficient as it yields almost 25 percent more energy than is used in growing the corn, harvesting it, and distilling it into ethanol. The most recent findings show that corn ethanol fuel is energy efficient and yields an energy output:input ratio of 1:6.

Biodiesel is a clean-burning, non-toxic, domestic, renewable fuel suitable for use in any diesel engine, without modification, and is made from natural oils, such as soybean oil. Biodiesel is made through a simple refining process called transesterification, and can be mass-produced in biorefineries or, with the right equipment, safely produced in small batches at home. Like ethanol, biodiesel can be blended into standard diesel fuel. The DOE has found that as the concentration of biodiesel increases, emissions of carbon monoxide, sulfates, particulates, unburned hydrocarbons and other pollutants are reduced. A full life cycle emissions study by the US DOE found that for every unit of fossil energy needed to make biodiesel, 3.2 units of energy are gained. Though far fewer gallons of biodiesel are produced than ethanol, its use is increasing much faster. The National Biodiesel Board reported 2006 biodiesel production at triple that of 2005.

Heat and Power

Unprocessed biomass, such as wood chips, hay or corn, can be combusted in a number of applications, on very large or very small scales, to produce clean and efficient heat

and power. Biomass may be direct-fired in power plants similar to standard fossil fuel firing plants, or co-fired by substituting biomass for a portion of coal. Economically, co-firing makes sense, as the existing equipment is often able to undergo minor adjustments to allow biomass, rather than requiring a new boiler designed exclusively for biomass combustion. Popular in Europe and the forest product industries, combined heat and power (CHP) projects burn biomass for electricity generation while capturing and utilizing the heat and steam produced, reaching incredible efficiencies. In biomass gasification, biomass is exposed to very hot temperatures in an environment where the solid biomass breaks down and forms a flammable gas, which is then used to produce electricity in a combined-cycle process that can reach 60% efficiency.

Biomass furnaces and stoves are installed systems that provide heat for a single building. Furnaces make use of existing ductwork of the building, delivering heat in the same way a traditional furnace does. Biomass stoves are stand-alone appliances, which move heat out of the stove into the surrounding space by an internal fan. Though there are several brands and many different models of corn and pellet stoves on the market, most have a similar design, which includes a hopper for fuel storage, an auger or similar mechanism of delivering the fuel to the firepot, ash or clinker storage, a gasket-sealed door to create negative pressurization needed for the fire, and an exhaust pipe and fan.

A Case Study:
The University of Iowa
Oat Hull Project.

In 2003 the University of Iowa pioneered a biomass co-firing program after being contacted about the sustainable disposal of oat hulls by a Quaker Oats plant 30 miles north of Iowa City. After a $1 million investment to add a storage silo and modify the power production system to accommodate the oat hulls, the University saves $500,000 per year by consuming 180 tons of oat hulls daily. Burning 30,000 fewer tons of coal annually, the University has reduced its CO_2 emissions by 72,000 tons, and sulfur emissions by 60 tons annually. The University is currently planning to expand the program.

Types of Biomass

Lignocellulosic biomass, commonly called cellulosic biomass, is made up of the fibrous parts of the plant like the leaves, stems and wood, as opposed to the grains and seeds. The cellulose and lignin within plant walls can either be broken down into fermentable sugar molecules in a process called hydrolysis, or the gases produced in gasification can be specially fermented. A final distillation of the fermented material produces ethanol. The cost of production will need to decline significantly before cellulosic ethanol becomes a widespread alternative fuel. There is no lack of incentive for research focused on increasing the conversion efficiency, as lignocellulose is perhaps the most abundant organic material on Earth.

Though it is important for soil quality and erosion control that a portion of the 500 million tons of **crop residue** produced each year remain in the fields, some residue, especially corn stover, are good candidates for use in helping meet our energy needs. The U.S. Department of Agriculture reports that up to 30% of surface residue can be removed from some no-till systems without increasing erosion or run-off, especially when other conservation farming practices, like contour planning, are employed. Crop residue can be baled for co-firing at power plants, pelleted for use in pellet stoves, or used as feedstock for cellulosic biomass.

The basic components of a kernel of **corn** are starch, protein, oil and fiber, which make it a versatile crop that is used in thousands of commercial products. In the United States, corn is the leading crop used to produce ethanol fuel for transportation. During the Depression, it was not uncommon to throw entire ears of corn, or just the bare cobs, into the wood stove for heat, but corn has not traditionally been known for its ability to produce warmth until recently. Today, dry feed corn, because it is naturally in pellet form, has widespread availability, high BTU content (see below) and renewability, is becoming a common fuel for heating homes in the Midwest and Northeast states.

Since **soybean oil** is the dominant oil produced in the U.S., the development of biodiesel has focused around soy oil. One bushel of soybeans produces about 1.5

gallons of biodiesel, according to Iowa State University's Soybean Extension and Research program.

Easily grown and extremely fermentable, **sugar** is even more efficiently converted to bioethanol than corn. Brazil, the largest sugar producing nation (13.9 million acres planted) is also the world leading exporter of ethanol, with over 330 sugar/ethanol mills, which produced 4 billion gallons of sugar ethanol in 2005, according to Gateway Brazil. One ton of sugarcane yields about 21 gallons of bioethanol when fermented and distilled. By burning the fibrous part of the sugarcane plant, **bagasse**, mills become energetically self-sufficient, producing the heat needed for distillation and electricity to run the mill. Burning bagasse has a low ash content of 2.5%, compared to 30-50% for coal combustion, and produces almost no nitrous oxides.

Millions of tons of wood scraps from lumber mills and forest-clearing can be turned into **wood pellets** and used as a renewable source of energy for heat. The Pellet Fuel Institute reports that 600,000 homes already heat with wood. Together, Sweden, Denmark and Austria consumed the vast majority of the world pellet fuel supply.

Poplar and **willow**, and other woody biomass species can be grown at high densities and coppice harvested at 3-4 year cycles, providing biomass for pellets or co-firing with coal for heat and electricity production. Growing and harvesting efficiently and as near as possible to the end use, as well as air-drying following harvest will further increase the environmental benefits of these carbon-neutral fuels.

Switchgrass is a tall, rapidly growing prairie grass native to central North America. Grown typically for ground cover, to provide wildlife areas, or to control erosion, it has recently become an attractive crop for cellulosic ethanol production. Due to higher ash production, switchgrass is less likely to be used for pellets at this time. Research using switchgrass-biomass combinations and stove development may make it a possibility in the future.

Already a commercial crop in Europe, **miscanthus** is a tall, rapidly growing tropical grass native to Africa and Asia. A University of Illinois study indicates that the high yield, low input, large root system, carbon sequestration and potential for wildlife cover make miscanthus an environmentally friendly crop.

The Energy in Corn

The energy content of dry corn is generally in the range of 8,000 to 8,500 BTU per pound. Because corn is not completely dry, the moisture content and other factors like the variety and cleanliness of the corn and weather patterns during growing and harvest must be taken into account.

Corn stoves generally require corn moisture content of 15% or less to operate. At this moisture level, a pound of corn would actually be composed of 0.85 lbs. of dry corn and 0.15 lbs. of water by weight. Assuming a median energy content of 8,250 BTUs per pound of dry corn, the energy content of one pound of corn with 15% moisture would be 7012.5 BTUs (8250 BTUs per pound of dry corn x 0.85 lb.).

Because energy is consumed in vaporizing the moisture in the corn we must subtract it from the amount of energy available to produce heat. Vaporizing one pound of water consumes 1,050 BTUs of energy, so vaporizing 0.15 lb. of water would consume 157.5 BTUs. Subtracting the energy of vaporization (7012.5 BTUs – 157.5BTUs) results in 6855 BTUs per pound.

The drier the corn you are burning, the greater amount of energy in the corn will be available to produce heat. The same calculations, with 11% moisture content would produce 7227 BTUs per pound, which add up over the course of a bushel, or a season's worth of corn to heat your home.

Balancing The Issue

The recent and continuing surge in utilizing crops for biomass energy has been possible, due in part to use of energy and chemicals in modern US agriculture. Does the energy used to produce corn outweigh the energy we gain from its end product?

Ethanol

Due to their energy intensiveness, early ethanol plants raised questions as to whether ethanol was worth the energy used to produce it.

A study published in *Science* magazine in January 2006 presented an evaluation of six analyses of corn-based ethanol. Analyses that reported negative net energy incorrectly ignored co-products (such as animal feed) and used obsolete data. Using co-products of ethanol offsets energy that would otherwise be used to produce the displaced products. All studies indicated that current corn ethanol technologies are much less petroleum-intensive than gasoline but have greenhouse gas emissions similar to those of gasoline.

The US Department of Agriculture released a study in 2005 that estimates the net energy balance of corn based on recent surveys of US corn producers and US ethanol plants. The results indicate that corn ethanol has a positive energy balance, even before subtracting the energy allocated to by-products. The net energy balance of corn ethanol adjusted for by-product credits is 27,729 and 33,196 BTU per gallon for wet- and dry-milling, respectively, and 30,528 BTU per gallon for the industry. The study results suggest that corn ethanol is energy efficient, as indicated by an energy output:input ratio of 1.67.

The most official US Department of Energy study of the issue, which also reviews other studies, concludes that the net energy balance of making fuel ethanol from corn grain is 1.34; that is, about one-third more energy as petroleum fuel. Cellulosic bioethanol from corn stover or other residue would have an even more favorable energy balance. For cellulosic bioethanol the US DOE study, based on growing and harvesting energy crops such as fast-growing trees, projects an energy balance of 2.62. A life-cycle analysis of producing ethanol from stover, currently underway, is expected to show a net energy ratio of more than 5. The energy ratio, or the net energy balance, is the ratio of energy produced to the energy consumed.

In fact, there are a number of studies showing that bio-based fuels are a net energy gain, and only very few that claim a negative balance. Why the discrepancy? The latter studies are using outdated data in their calculations, and don't factor co-products into the equation. Ethanol production today requires about 50 percent less energy than in the early 1980s. During this same period, ethanol yields have increased by more than 22 percent, from 2.2 gallons per bushel of corn to 2.7 gallons per bushel, according to the US DOE. Recent leaps in the efficiency of both agriculture and ethanol production make the energy ratio much more favorable. Still more energy gain comes from generating electricity by burning the co-product lignin.

Corn and Pellet stoves

Because of recent focus on agricultural energy efficiency, including more widespread use of practices such as alternative tillage systems, producing an acre of corn consumes less energy than it once did. Many farmers are using less petroleum-based fertilizers and pesticides per acre and many farms are finding profitability in organics. The US Department of Agriculture reported in 2002 that the acreage of American farmlands under organic management, and growing major crops like corn and soybeans, doubled between 1992 and 1997, and again between 1997 and 2001. Many of the Midwest corn belt states are in the lead in terms

In the future, pelletized fuels and corn may be delivered in bulk directly to the storage area at your home. In fact, Bixby Energy Systems is working to build just such an infrastructure that would be scalable to local communities, similar to a water softener salt delivery system. In the area around Iowa City, IA, customers of Century Farm Harvest Heat have corn delivered and efficiently blown into their bulk storage container.

of total certified organic cropland, driving corn's energy ratio well into the range that makes it a viable choice.

Modern corn and pellet stoves are carefully engineered to burn granular fuel at a high combustion efficiency, the ability to produce useful heat, and are continually improving. There are stoves on the market today with combustion efficiencies as high as 99.7%.

Pellets made with stover, sunflower hulls or other would-be waste products involve consumption of only the energy to transport the biomass, the energy to pelletize and the energy consumed to produce a bag, if one is used. Because pelleted material is not usually produced specifically for pelletization, the energy it produces is a bonus.

Finally, local fuel is efficient. Consider the energy utilized in drilling, refining and pumping or mining and shipping fossil fuels around the globe or across a continent for heat as compared to the energy it takes to transport corn from a farm 10 miles away, or pellets made from waste biomass in your region.

EQUIVALENT HEATING VALUES

Fuel Currently Used	Equal to	Pounds of Shelled Corn
1 ton of Hard Coal	=	3,360
1 gallon of #2 Fuel Oil	=	22
1,000,000 BTU of Natural Gas	=	170
1 gallon of Propane	=	15
1 full cord of Firewood	=	2,800
1 ton of Wood Pellets	=	2,575
1,000 kWh of Electricity	=	635

All graphs and energy values provided with permission of Dennis Buffington, "Energy Selector," 20 January 2006, <http://energy.cas.psu.edu/energyselector/> (5 September 2006).

the feel-good heat

The Burners

So many questions, "What does it burn? Will it heat my house? Does it smell? Is it dirty? Where will I get corn and where should I keep it? Does the corn pop when you burn it?"

The following interviews are intended to share a glimpse of life with a corn or pellet stove through answering questions like those listed above and sharing challenges and advice. The interviewees make up a diverse group of 25, both families and businesses that have heated with a biomass stove for at least one winter, including a monk, a millionaire, city people, rural folks, young families and grandparents, a musician, a teacher, bankers and an auto parts store.

Though each stove experience is unique, you will find similarities in their stories, attitudes and enthusiasm for burning biomass. Many say they would continue to burn corn or biomass pellets even if natural gas or liquid propane became cheaper. Why? This group of modern day pioneers values replacing fossil fuels with a renewable fuel that is clean burning and carbon neutral. They are proud to support their local economies, turning what may end up as waste into a valuable fuel to keep their families and customers warm throughout the winter.

Meet the pioneers in corn and biomass energy…

Maggie & Glen Mowery

Location: Iowa City, IA (urban)
Square footage—1600 sq. ft.

How many winter seasons have you used a corn stove?

Maggie: We used it last winter during construction on the house. There were holes around the windows and cold air coming in, so we ran it constantly.

Glen: For the last half of the winter, the corn stove heated the house by itself.

Do you remember the first time you heard of corn stoves? What was your first reaction?

Maggie: It was his idea, but I fell in love with it.

Glen: A friend from work bought one a few years ago, and I got a good chuckle out of it. He came into work and said, "Hey, I bought a corn stove," and I said, "Ah, I'm truly in Iowa now. We're burning corn." Then he kept telling me how much he liked it.

What were the deciding factors in buying a corn stove?

Glen: It was a combination of things. Our furnace downstairs isn't real old, but it's got some age to it, and we were wondering if it was time to replace it. Well, we thought if we had a corn stove we would have an alternate heat source if we lost our primary heater in the winter. And it didn't cost as much as a replacement furnace, so we thought we'd give it a try to see if we liked it. Another reason to delay replacing the furnace is that we have an old hand-dug well that I am thinking of using for a ground source heat pump.

Ah, I'm truly in Iowa now. We're burning corn.

Why is corn a better choice for you than natural gas or wood?

Glen: Energy is my business, so it's neat to have a renewable heat source. I was in a little bit of a quandary though, because we're burning a feed source as well. So it somehow didn't seem right to be burning corn. But if you compare it to oil, natural gas and other fossil fuels, it makes more sense. That's why I was pretty excited to hear that they're moving towards pelletized corncob, where you're truly getting waste product. But still it's nice to be burning something renewable. And the wildlife loves it when we spill corn on the way to the house.

Describe how your corn stove works.

Glen: It's gravity feed out of the hopper. An auger moves the corn horizontally into the combustion chamber and as it burns there's a separate auger that rotates every few minutes, just enough to stir the corn. That's what gives it that nice big flame and also breaks up clinkers.

What reactions have you had from non-Midwest family and friends?

Glen: People kind of question it a little bit. When I went back East for the holidays I was talking about it and people looked at me funny.

Maggie: Usually you have to give an explanation of what "burning corn" means, because they say, "What do you mean, corn? Corn cob?"

How do people visiting the house react to the corn stove?

Glen: Everybody thinks it's pretty neat. I think that's the common reaction.

Maggie: We've had lots of construction people through here because we're still in the remodeling process with the house. All those guys think it's really great and they're surprised at how much heat it gives out.

Glen: This model produces more heat than other types of corn stoves. It supplies good radiant heat in addition to the convective heat. When it's at full flame, you can't stand to put your hand on the stove. It's quite warm. It would be a drawback for families with kids. But those cold days when you're chilled to the bone you can appreciate the radiant heat.

What do you think of corn stoves as a financial investment?

Glen: Corn stoves aren't exactly cheap. It would take several years to pay back a corn stove.

Maggie: Our monthly cost right now is less than natural gas heating costs.

Glen: The way natural gas prices are going, this becomes more and more attractive.

What advice would you give someone considering a corn stove for his or her home?

Maggie: I don't think it pays to buy a less expensive corn stove because of the amount of messing you have to do with it in terms of getting it started.

Glen: Do your homework. There are so many different units out there. Some are very simplistic; other models detect room temperature and adjust the heat output according the setpoint. A few models have electric start up, other models take manual starter fluid to start the fire.

Have you had any problems with your corn stove?

Maggie: Occasionally, if you turn it off and the hopper is full, when you turn it on again, it turns more corn on an already full auger, and it won't start up again. So we've had to dig out the corn. This may be due to corn moisture content, but we don't know for sure.

Glen: The blower wasn't working when the unit was first started up. You could feel the heat coming off it, but it wasn't forced air. It was a relatively minor problem that was corrected. We had it puff a few times when attempting to ignite and put pressure back up through the exhaust. There was no sustained flame, just a pressure pop.

Do you feel safe with the corn stove in the house?

Glen: Oh yes, we can leave it on every day.

Maggie: We leave the house with it on. It's very contained and enclosed.

What was you're biggest surprise upon heating with your stove?

Maggie: How much heat it actually put out. We didn't shut our furnace off; we just set it down to 65 degrees. It never ran and that was just shocking.

Glen: We're able to keep the house much warmer now than we did with just natural gas.

How much time did you spend maintaining the stove last winter?

Glen: It takes about 10 minutes to bring in 2 buckets of corn.

Maggie: You have to be strong to bring in the buckets, that's the thing.

Glen: Emptying the ash from the hopper every third day is the bigger pain, because you can't empty the ash without making a mess, and it's hot. And then you need to vacuum the ash out occasionally, which helps with efficiency.

Where do you see the future of corn stoves and biomass energy?

Glen: I think there's an opportunity with feed stock, to genetically engineer corn for extra big kernels with very high BTU content. Not as a food product, but specifically as an energy source.

What other forms of biomass do you think could be burned as fuel?

Glen: Oat hulls are being burned at the University of Iowa. I'm not a big fan of wood pellets right now because of the energy it takes to create the pellet. It takes away from the renewability of the product when it takes energy to process the fuel. I do like the idea of corncob pellets because that's otherwise a waste product.

How are you affecting the environment by burning corn?

Glen: Burning corn is a carbon neutral process, so the carbon that it gives off when it is burned is carbon that was absorbed during its growing process. However, there are still emissions associated with planting, harvesting and transporting the corn.

Ode to my corn stove....

Its heat keeps me warm,
its flame relaxes,
while helping local farmers,
it's good for the masses.

I feed it and clean it,
and fuel it with more,
while throwing the clinkers
outside of my door.

It's good for the earth,
a renewable source,
why look to foreign
    countries?,
is my question, of course.

Warm up your heart,
your soul and your home,
buy a Harvest Heat
    corn stove,
and ye shall never roam!

Mary Audia, 2006
Coralville, IA

33

Prusha Napa Auto
Connie Prusha

Location: West Liberty, IA (urban)

Number of winter seasons with corn stove: 2

Time before payback of initial investment: 1 year

Corn or pellet: corn

What square footage of your business is heated by your corn stove?

Over 1800 square feet. The only insulation we have is in the ceiling, and the corn stove provides a steady, comfortable heat.

What were the deciding factors in buying a corn stove?

This building here is not insulated very well at all. The previous bills for the gas had been extremely high, usually $386-$440 per month. So I decided we had to do something different, especially with the price of gas going up. The initial investment seemed a little high, but based on my first bill, I think mine's going to pay for itself in about a year. We paid $1.30 per bushel of corn and only went through a bushel a day, so with a corn stove, we're only spending $45 per month on heat.

Describe the temperature of your shop before and after installing the corn stove?

The year we just used gas, people would not stay in here because it was so cold. I kept it between 60 and 62 in here because of the price of gas. It stays between 70 and 72 in here now, which is fine, and you have to remember the doors are constantly opening and shutting. But it's nice to walk into a store that's warm and toasty. Now people will come in and loiter.

Why do you choose to burn corn rather than natural gas? Or wood?

The house we just moved out of had a fireplace. We would put wood in the fire at night and either wake up in the middle of the night to put more wood in, or wake up in the morning and there was no fire and it was cold. And knowing that all you have to do is once every 24 hours dump a bag of corn that weighs 40 lbs. into this and walk away, that's just so nice.

What reservations did you have about switching to corn heat?

The only thing we were concerned about was that if we lose electricity, we'll lose heat. Well, if you have electric heat, you'll also lose heat. That's why we still have gas heat as a backup.

Describe the first few weeks with your stove.

There was maintenance, but it was like getting anything else, a new computer, a new program, learning how it functions. A corn stove is not something you're going to know how to do in 30 seconds; it's going to take a little while. The first stove we had would plug up occasionally, but we wouldn't call for help every time, we'd just deal with it, fix it ourselves. But when Ed found out, he hooked me up with a different stove, and the first week with that was just awesome.

Describe the daily routine with your stove.

All you do is light up with ½ cup full of pellets, a little fire starter, make sure there's corn in the hopper, shut the door and start it up. We would fill it up with corn at 3:00 in the afternoon, come in and drop the clinker at 9:00 the next morning, and not fill it again until 3:00 that afternoon. It's just a normal routine like anything else. It's no different than getting up in the morning and brushing your teeth, and you pick the time you want to do it. It really wasn't a routine we go into, it was really just a part of opening and closing the store.

35

Where do you store your corn?

We have a gravity wagon outside. I would just load up a bag of corn, bring it in, and dump it.

What advice would you give someone considering a corn stove for heating?

For businesses that are in a pinch and want their customers to be comfortable, I'd say this is it. I'd even say, "Here, take mine for a week." I would say go for it, there's no loss in it at all.

How do you keep mice out of your corn?

We did have mice at first, but we found a cure and have never had another mouse: mothballs. Put the corn on a pallet and scatter mothballs.

Describe customer reaction. What is their first impression?

We have a lot of people who are interested in it, especially because of the price of fuel. It's relaxing and it gives a beautiful flame. They like it due to the fact that it's practically maintenance free and it's inexpensive. A bushel of corn doesn't take up much room. There's a lot of interest.

What do your children think of your corn stove?

I remember my youngest son asking me why I was wasting my money. He's been in the store, and now he's going to put one in his house.

How safe do you perceive your corn stove?

It has so many safety features. The first safety feature that I liked was that the sides don't get hot, because I have kids coming in here. The glass does get hot, but you can avoid that by letting the kids know. The other safety feature is that if the door is left open for 45 seconds the fire will go out. So I never felt any concern at all, and we do keep chemicals up there near the stove. Our insurance company said they can insure my building with a corn burner, but could not insure it if it was a fireplace. If my insurance company were to ever tell me that I couldn't have a corn stove, I would drop my insurance. I think that it's the safest, most economical, money-saving choice.

Corn and pellet stoves are becoming popular in public locations as well. In eastern Iowa there are stoves now placed in the cities of Marion, Iowa City, Coralville and West Liberty. The stove above is located at the new Johnson County Iowa Historical Society Museum. Executive Director Margaret Weiting says, "The first impression for visitors to the Johnson County Historical Society Museum in Coralville, Iowa is the Lobby. The St. Croix corn burning stove adds a WOW! factor to the ambience of this setting. Part of the JCHS' mission is to share the connection between the past-present-future and the belief that we build our future by understanding our past. The stove is a great pointer to these connections."

What's burning with ...

Carolyn Zaiser

Location: Iowa City (urban)
Square feet heated with corn stove: 2100 zero lot
Seasons with corn stove: 2
Corn or pellets: corn

How is your corn stove set up in you house?

It's downstairs, and I live upstairs. It vents through the chimney in my fireplace and it didn't take long at all to set up. When it gets really cold I do have to put a standing fan on the landing to shoot the warm air up here.

What appealed to you about burning corn for heat?

I just like the whole concept. I just don't think we should be dependent on oil any longer. Corn is clean burning and good for the environment. I like the idea of living closer to the land. I think getting back to the basics is so much better.

What was the deciding factor in buying a corn stove?

I figured my payback. They say with any energy-saving device that you're looking to buy, if the payback is under 5 years, go for it. Mine was 3.5.

How warm do you keep your house in the winter?

I went through the corn a little faster, because I keep it cranked up a little higher than most people would because the stove is downstairs. I like it cool in the wintertime anyway; 67 degrees is too hot for me. Sometimes it would get too warm in here and I'd have to open a window.

How much money have you saved?

During normal gas price years I would typically pay about $110-120 per month. Imagine [what I would have paid] this last year when gas prices went up. During the 3-4 months I had the corn stove, I paid only $40 which included the gas for my stove and water heater. Talk about amazing. What a savings. And I don't think gas prices are going to get any better.

Where did you store your corn?

Actually, in new garbage cans. They (Century Farm Harvest Heat) just take them, fill them up, drop them off. I haul them inside and that's it.

What sort of reaction have you had from friends and co-workers?

People at work are so funny because I told them all about it; they called me Corn Queen. They quit laughing and giving me a bad time when I told them what my bills were.

My boss said, "Oh for crying out loud, just flip the switch, you make enough money to pay for the gas." I said, "No, that's not the point, I don't want to spend my money on that. I want to spend it on travel and other things." I don't mind doing a little work; it's 5 minutes. It's good for you.

How does it feel to be a pioneer of the energy world?

It's interesting—I didn't realize I was. I'm pleased I ran across it because I think I'm contributing to hopefully making a difference in our environment. I think that's the thing to do. I've changed my life and am trying to do the things that are right, like using compact fluorescent bulbs. I'm just trying to do what I can.

Describe your maintenance routine.

It's a teeny little stove with all that heat coming out of it and it's so easy to clean. I just take my fireplace brush and clean the inside good, the walls, the grates, use the grate cleaner, clean the ash out and that's it. The only thing I did regularly was pull out a little stick that drops the ash out of the ventilation fan. You can get about 1 or 2 clinkers per day. To me, this is very low maintenance. And I would fill the hopper twice a day.

What sort of problems or maintenance trouble did you have?

The clinker was solid as a rock. I couldn't cut through it unless I caught it at exactly the right time. Ed said it might be the way the corn grew this year. Also, if the fire goes out it's like 20 minutes until you can start a new one. I found a way to drop the clinker so the fire didn't go out, so that's not such an issue anymore.

What other advice would you like to share?

To people with no understanding of something like this, you just have to start thinking outside the box because this makes so much sense. So there are two sides of it, if you're just money-conscious, great, fantastic. But if you're environmentally-conscience too, and aware, it's something to think about. We all need to move toward alternative fuels. Whether that's in our cars or in our homes.

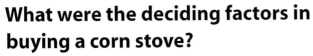

Jim Heineman

Owner, The Fancy Street Light Company, Inc.,
Rock Island, Illinois
Corn or pellets: corn
Number of stoves: 3
Number of winters with corn stoves: 2
(2005-2006)
Square feet heated: 21,000 square feet

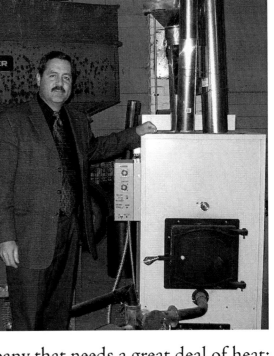

What were the deciding factors in buying a corn stove?

To stop being held hostage to the local utility company and the natural gas prices. We're a company that needs a great deal of heat; we heat a large area. My previous natural gas bill in 2004 just clobbered me. I needed an additional heating system in the outer shop, and I had a local heating and air conditioning specialist come in and tell me I needed a $15,000 unit and I needed to run a larger gas line to it, because of how much gas it was going to consume. And that's when I decided that rather than spending $8000 on running additional gas lines on top of the huge cost of natural gas, to look at this corn thing seriously.

You've kept very accurate records of natural gas and electric usage, as well as financial savings. Describe the trends you see.

We used 4835 thermal units of natural gas in October, Nov. and Dec. in 2004, without corn stoves. For the same period in 2005—that's only with 2 units, we didn't get our third unit until January of 2006—we went down to 2322 thermal units. And that's still deceiving because some of that was used by our renters, who occupy 30,000 square feet in another part of the building, and heat using only natural gas. So this year we will have a separate gas meter and I fully expect that our gas usage will decrease by 90%.

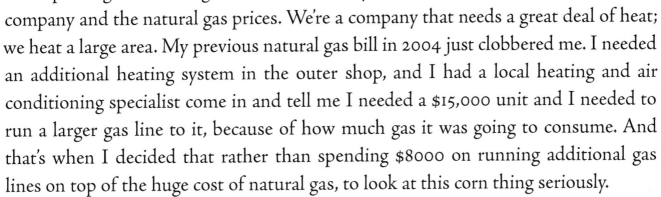

In 2004 keep in mind though that it was only .71¢ per thermal unit. That jumped in 2005, the rate went from $.71 to $1.11. My bill in 2004 was $2900 just for natural gas just for those three months. My bill in 2005 was only $2577. (Again that includes my renter, so the numbers are really skewed badly.) If you take the 2322 thermal units times the old rate to get a fair comparison—on an even unit cost—that would've saved me $1643 in three months if natural gas price in 2005 would've been the same price as in 2004. Since they went up, I saved even more.

I also wanted to look at the kilowatt-hours though. We just went with standard zone heating which works fine if you want to do it low tech. I was just concerned that by leaving the blowers on pretty much continuously we would lose a lot of savings by increasing our kilowatt-hours. In fact, our kilowatt-hours were lower by about 15%. I don't entirely know what I can attribute that to, but the blowers obviously must use very little electricity, so it was a win-win.

	2004	2005
Cost per BTU	.71¢	$1.11
BTUs used	4035	2322
Oct-Dec heating bill	$2900	$2577

We'll start a very good monitoring system starting in October, knowing to the dollar exactly what our gas and electrical costs are. We're going to add one more unit in the outer shop just to raise the temperature a little more. My belief is that we'll cut our costs by 90%.

Have you calculated the payback on your investment?

If I calculate out our renters, I know we paid for more than one unit in a year, about 1.3 units. I think if we have a hard winter this year—and we have them running right away in October—I'll have my investment back in 2 years. You can talk to any banker in America; any investment that pays for its self in 2 years is a good decision.

What would you tell other business owners about heating using corn stoves?

If we would not have had the corn stoves, with the huge increase in natural gas per thermal unit last year and coming into this year, our gas bill would have doubled. Armed with the right numbers, I can't imagine why a business owner wouldn't do this, unless the owner just has so much money they don't care. I really can't see why anyone, even with only 2 or 3 employees wouldn't do this, because you can always find 20 minutes during the day for one or two of your employees to take care of it and the savings are tremendous. So again, to me, I can't really understand why any small, midsize or even large company would not take a look at this.

Referred to as the "cube" Harvest Heat provides these for customers that are on a regular fuel delivery program. These cubes are easy to maintain and hold about thirty-two bushels of corn. They provide an easy pouring spout for access.

Meggitt Household—

Alisa, Josh, James & Uncle Steve
Location: Iowa City (rural)
Square feet: 2000
Winters with a corn stove: 2
Corn or pellets: corn

How does it feel being a pioneer of the energy world?

Alisa: It's so much fun. It feels like finally I get to be aligned. I feel like I have a link to the future now. Presently we'll profit and in the future James will profit.

Describe your house before heating with corn.

Alisa: We were keeping it cool because gas prices were so high. We would freeze. It's a big, leaky house, and we kept it at 48 degrees (Fahrenheit) sometimes. I couldn't stand to be there. There were times when you could see your breath in our bedroom.

How was your house different this winter?

Alisa: We crank it up now, we wear short sleeves, and our guests actually take off their coats. It's balmy, warm, it's nice. We knocked internal walls out which really opened the house up. We strategically place fans but the heat doesn't get all the way to the east wing. We're really impressed with the performance so far.

Tell me about your stove.

Josh: It's a St. Croix, it holds about a bushel of corn. We fill it about once every 24 hours or so. The outside doesn't get savagely hot, where you'd get roasted if you were to touch it, but the heat coming out of the stove is about 120 degrees or so, so it's really blasting the heat out. We also like it because it doesn't take up a huge chunk of space in the house. It can be close to the walls as opposed to a wood-burning stove, which has to be a few feet away.

Why is burning corn a good choice for your family?

Alisa: I'm an environmentalist; he's a penny-pincher, so our values aligned through that.

When did you first hear of corn stove?

Josh: A co-worker of mine has had one for a few years. So we knew they were out there for a number of years. We didn't really get serious about it until gas prices really shot up.

Alisa: I heard a radio spot and wrote the number down.

Describe your corn stove maintenance.

Uncle Steve: I fill the corn stove in the morning and evening.

Josh: It's easy to maintain, requires maybe 5 minutes or so each day.

Uncle Steve, what do you think of the corn stove?

Uncle Steve: I like the smell of the corn. I think it's efficient and it helps cut down costs. Global warming has gotten to be an increasingly more important issue, particularly in the last 5-10 years. Emissions of CO_2 are one of the larger culprits of global warming, and the corn stove doesn't contribute as much. Coal and oil are the biggest.

How safe do you perceive your corn stove?

Josh: Mark (see page 68) explained it really well, how safe it really is. Even when we open it up there's no flame blasting out.

Alisa: A lot of people have expressed concerns about fire issues, but 100% of the time it's about wood burning stoves. It really is a perception. People have said, "Oh, you're going to have rats and snakes and things in your house, it's going to catch on fire."

What problems have you had with your stove?

Josh: There were nails that jammed the auger, but we were able to take those out. We had to take all the corn out and were able to take the nail out with pliers.

Alisa: One problem is that corn is going to be much more expensive this year. Last year it was $200 all winter. This year it will be $60 per month if we pick it up. But comparing oil and corn prices is like apples and oranges.

WE WOULD FREEZE

How do you justify burning corn, a feed and export crop?

Alisa: I'd rather use it for heat than to feed cows to feed people. It's a more efficient use. I've had a PhD from Cornell say that with the whole environmental life cycle inputs it's no better than anything else, with all the fuel that goes into transporting and harvesting. My counter to that is that it's not being shipped from 6000 miles away, it's not costing the US $1 billion a day of military effort, it's not as much blood.

How do you view the environmental aspects of burning corn?

Alisa: When I was in the Peace Corps living in the desert in sub-Saharan Africa, we lived through 2 droughts. My friends there lived off the land; you go and harvest your food and that's what you store and eat for a year. If you have one harvest per year and it doesn't rain that year that means you have no food. So I watched kids and old people and animals starve. It really affected me a lot. I think Iowa farmland is the most precious commodity in Iowa. We have 10% of the world's richest farmland. We lose 26,000 acres of it every year to urban sprawl and poor development patterns. I'm thrilled that this is a way to keep that farmland in production and add value to those farmers trying to make a living off of working the land. I see it that profoundly.

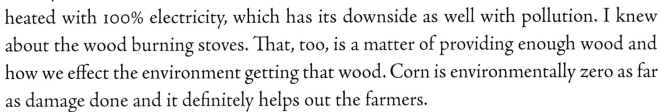

Father Anthony Good

Location: Watertown, WI (rural)
Pellet, or Corn: Corn
Number of winters with a
corn stove: 2

Why do you choose to heat your home with corn rather than natural gas or wood?

Mainly because it's cleaner. In the 80s I heated with 100% electricity, which has its downside as well with pollution. I knew about the wood burning stoves. That, too, is a matter of providing enough wood and how we effect the environment getting that wood. Corn is environmentally zero as far as damage done and it definitely helps out the farmers.

When do you remember first hearing about corn stoves?

The issue of energy awareness must have been back almost to the Carter era, when the oil embargo took place. In the 90s I heard about the corn burners, and I thought to myself, "We seem to have been going down the wrong road, making ourselves dependent on foreign oil."

What fueled your interest in corn stoves?

Besides the environmental benefits, it was a financial decision. Raising 47 foster children over my lifetime, finances were quite a chore. It's about the children I've raised and their children and the legacy I leave. I do believe we have a responsibility to take care of what God has given us. Not just as if it is our own, but knowing it is on loan and is going to be returned to God. I'd like to feel that I've returned to God what he's given me, in better shape than when I got it.

What's burning with ...

How have your finances changed since you've started heating with corn?

The last year before I had a corn stove I paid $4700 on oil. Just to fill the tank up for 3 weeks would have been $700. Cost-wise, there was no way I was going to survive. My furnace was almost new, but ended up breaking. The company had gone out of business and I couldn't get them to replace the parts. So I sat myself down and did some praying. I now spend an average of $387 per month on corn. Last year I ordered 8000 lbs. of corn for heating, which will last all through the summer as feed for the geese, goats, chickens and pigeons.

What particular challenges have you had with your corn stove?

The first six weeks were tricky. There were some real problems with starting up, but most of them were caused by lack of knowledge on my part. The directions are more geared toward people who know what they're doing. The terminology was hard, the names of different components, and I had no idea what they were talking about. Once I tried to solve some of the problems by trial and error, the problems took care of themselves gradually.

How many people do you know who also have corn stoves?

Only the guy that comes to service mine. I think a lot of people are interested in them, but I think a lot of people are scared of the work, which I don't understand. So many people get into the car, go to the health spa, walk on the treadmill for an hour. You can spend more time doing that than I do going outside to bring the corn in.

Where do you get your corn, and how do you store it?

From a co-op, and I ask for sifted corn, which works best. I use a 200 gallon plastic trash can that keeps the corn outside dry enough. In the winter I wait for a warmer day, and then fill the bins inside, which hold 1000 lbs. and 600 lbs. I usually spend 3 hours per month working with the corn.

Has your corn stove changed your life at home or how you spend time there?

Yes, the kitchen used to be the center. Now, with the flame burning in the stove, the dining room is much more comfortable. It's a nice place to sit and have a cup of coffee or read. When people come by for spiritual advice, it's a much more homelike atmosphere to sit and relax. A natural flame has a soothing effect. It gives the room a different atmosphere altogether.

Why do you think corn produces so much heat?

Because God gave it to us for that reason, besides eating. George Washington Carver's quote is prophetic. We need to clean up our own act. We should start asking what we can do for our country to become less dependent on foreign oil.

How are you affecting the environment by burning corn?

There aren't pollutants going out of my chimney anymore. It's cleaner for my animals and for everyone else.

How warm was your house on average last winter?

On almost the lowest setting the temperature in the house stays at 74. It's almost too warm for myself. I used to keep everything at 66.

What else do you think could be run on corn?

I presume corn could be used for those people who use air conditioning. Hot water tanks, definitely. It could be used to run a generator or lighting. Stuff like that would be very, very helpful, especially for people who live in the country.

What other forms of biomass do you think could be burned as fuel?

I think almost any of the seed products could be. Wheat, oats; we just have not done the research. I think people got greedy making money off of oil.

Any other thoughts?

I consider Ed and his staff heroes in the energy world as far as how god intended us to use it. They've helped me get back to my roots, as far as my vow of poverty and using materials wisely, and ridding myself of some impatience that I didn't even know I had.

Night Creature

I love the dying time of the year
When the fields are quiet
The leaves wave one last long
    good-bye
And the North Wind runs in
    like a riot
Of delightfully wicked children

I love driving home through the
    darkening
When only the sky is brilliant
I feel so safe, so protected
Slipping in and out of shadows
    like a phantom
Wrapped snug in the cloak of
    night
So nothing can harm me

I come home to warmth and fire
The merry ping of the corn stove
    greets me at the door
Like an eager pup
I fill its hopper, and pat its lid
Then pour myself a glass of wine
    dark red, dark as it comes
And sink down to savor the
    lengthening night

Gayla D. Paul, 2006
Iowa City, IA

the feel-good heat

What's burning with ...

Pam and Jerry Ausman

Location: Fairfield, IA (urban)
Corn or pellets: corn
Number of winters with corn stove: 2
Dollars saved on fuel during 2005-2006
winter season: $700

When did you first encounter the idea of burning corn for heat? What was your first reaction?

Pam: I'd read up on corn and pellet stoves and knew that a corn stove was what I wanted. For two years I'd wanted a corn stove, and Jerry will verify that. Jerry was a little reticent at first. But when the energy prices were going to be really high last winter, we started shopping around.

Why do you choose to burn corn?

Pam: I just really want to be not dependent on foreign oil, and we want to use renewable fuel. Jerry and I just really thought it was the thing to do.

Jerry: A wood stove is cheap, but it's so much work. The corn is a lot less work. It's a lot cleaner and easier.

Pam: The difference between a corn stove and a wood stove is like day and night.

How well does your corn stove heat your house?

Jerry: It can heat the entire thing, except when it's really cold. There's a fan on the stove that circulates the air.

Describe the temperature of your house before and after installing the corn stove.

Pam: We used to keep it about 74 degrees. It stays about 80-82 degrees in this room all the time now. The rest of the house stays between 70 and 75. We also kept it warmer later in the spring than we would have if we were heating with gas.

Jerry: In the spring we just fired it up at night and shut it off during the daytime.

How much money did you save last year on heating costs?

Pam: Not factoring the cost of the stove, we saved over $700 last winter, and it was a mild winter.

Describe any problems you've had with your stove.

Pam: We first got a stove from the local farm supply store, and we had nothing but problems with it. We were going along thinking, "Boy this is going to be a lot of work," because it put out a coffee can full of fly ash 3 times per day. I cleaned it out in the morning and afternoon and Jerry cleaned it out at night.

As it got colder, we had to put it on higher heat, and I noticed there was soot on the table; it was blowing ash into the house. I said to Jerry, "This is not acceptable."

Jerry: First we talked to Century Farm Harvest Heat to make sure we could get another stove. Then we approached the feed store about returning the stove.

Pam: The good thing is that after such a bad experience, we had such a good experience with the new stove. It was like night and day, we were just ecstatic.

How much time did you spend on average hauling corn and maintaining your stove per week or month last winter?

Pam: On average we spend about 15 minutes a day on the corn stove.

Jerry: We drop the clinker once a day, and it's so easy. I shut it down once a week to clean it out, which is the only time we shut it down. You don't need to do this, but I clean the corn to get all the excess cobs and leaves out. I can clean enough corn to last me a week in about an hour. It's just such an efficient stove. It's friendly; it works with you and you work with it.

Describe reactions of visitors to your home. What was their first impression?

Jerry: People are amazed. They'll come in and ask us how much do we get out of a bushel of corn, and they they'll just amazed how 8 or 10 kernels will drop in there and it will just flame up. Everybody who comes over likes to stand right in front of it and get warm.

How safe do you perceive your corn stove?

Pam: It only gets hot to the touch only on the front and top, but nothing like a wood stove. Our insurance company charged us $40 more because we had a corn stove. We changed over to another company that doesn't charge us more, and they shouldn't. Because really, it's really safe. It's not going to get out of control.

Jerry: It can't get out of control. If the electricity goes out, the fire will go out. If it runs out of corn the fire will go out. If the door is open over 30 seconds it goes out.

Pam: It's safer than anything. We need to educate our insurance companies.

How do you acquire and store corn?

Jerry: We have a gravity flow wagon that holds over 125 bushels in the garage that we filled up at the local feed store. We got 110 bushels for $1.78 each and that lasted us almost the whole winter. We used about 190 bushels total.

What advice would you give someone considering a corn stove for his or her home?

Pam: One thing people should be aware of is to investigate, and really talk to people about how the stove should run. Cheaper is not always better.

Albert Dose

Also in household:
Wife, Kathryn
Location: Lostant, IL (rural)
Corn or pellets: corn
Square footage: 1200
Winters with corn stove: 4

How well does the corn stove heat your home?

We built a new house a year and a half ago. The new house is very energy efficient with an open design. We have ceiling fans running to circulate the heat. It stays in the upper 70s up to about 80s in here. I'd keep it about 5 degrees cooler if I was paying for gas. An LP gas stove furnace is built in as a back up to the corn stove.

When did you first encounter the idea of burning corn for heat?

My oldest boy got interested in corn stoves first. We saw them at a farm show in Peoria and liked it.

Why do you choose to burn corn rather than natural gas?

I'm a big believer in conservation. We're using a renewable source of energy that to the farmer isn't worth very much when it's in surplus. LP gas is so expensive and surplus corn is worth almost nothing, so you might as well burn it.

How do you store corn?

We store it in a covered side-dump wagon that we keep close to the house. I go out every day or so to get more corn. The corn does burn better if you keep it in the house for a day or so before burning it.

How many people do you know who also have corn stoves?

Probably half a dozen. I've been around 3 other brands and I prefer this one by far, for a lot of reasons. It's fairly simple to maintain.

How much corn do you go through in a week?

We'd burn 2 to 3 5-gallon buckets/day. We used about 150 bushels of corn last heating season. I know we would have used about 2-500 gal tanks of LP gas at 1.92/gallon. There's a big savings there. Last year I used 10% out of the tank for the hot water heater, and heating 7-8 days out of the winter.

Describe any problems you've had with your stove.

Several gear blocks have gone bad on the feeding wheel. They were replaced because it was under warranty.

It goes without saying that any fireplace, heater or stove can be dangerous if not used properly, however, children and stove users all seem to agree, corn and pellet stoves are extremely safe and efficient as shown by Lohman R. Provorse, age 3.

What's burning with ...

Bob and Karen Dose

Location: Lostant, IL (rural)
Corn or Pellets: Corn
Number of winters with a corn stove: 4
Square footage heated: 1200

When did you first encounter the idea of burning corn for heat?

Bob: We first saw a Bixby corn stove at the 2000 farm show in Peoria, IL. I was very intrigued by the possibility of a corn stove helping lessen the cost of our heating bill. We did some research on the different models and decided to go with the Bixby 100. We chose the Bixby 100 because of its high efficiency, sleek style, and the aesthetic value of watching the fire on cold nights.

Why does burning corn to heat your home make sense for you?

Karen: We chose burning corn because of the economics of burning corn over propane and the availability of corn.

Bob: Out of all the alternative fuels to heat a home, corn burning made sense. There is very little preparation and no long hours of intensive work that seemingly never ends. You just fill the hopper then press the start button.

How did you adjust to the first several weeks with a corn stove?

Karen: It was like having a fireplace that was easily maintained. I really liked that.

Bob: When we first bought the stove there were some minor adjustments that needed to be made. Once we were able to work out the kinks we both were excited at how easy it was and how little our propane furnace was turning on. The stove was able to keep our home at a comfortable temperature. Anyone can take care of a Bixby because it is so simple to operate and maintain. It was so simple to operate my father

the feel-good heat

decided to buy one. He keeps the temperature comfortable in his new home and has been able to save on energy costs.

What are the biggest benefits to burning corn?

Bob: Keeping our money in the USA and not contributing to the pollution and reduction of our non-renewable resources by burning biomass. It's a little work, but it's worthwhile and gives us a nice warm house. One five gallon bucket heats our home for about 3 days on the coolest setting. On real cold days we set the stove to 3 (out of 8) where a five-gallon bucket lasts almost 2 days. The efficiency is impressive.

How do you acquire and store corn?

Bob: We wait until the corn is naturally dried down (15%-14%) in the field and then I take the corn right from our corn field, so it has little foreign material. The grain goes straight to wagon from the combine. I then place a tarp over the wagon and I store it for the year.

Describe any problems you've had with your stove?

Bob: I vented the corn stove through the roof and had some problems with the exhaust of the stove. I got a new pipe and vented it horizontally out the house from behind the stove. It now operates better then ever.

Karen: When it rained or snowed the pipe would let moisture in to the stove and we had to keep adjusting the airflow.

Bob: We also found that with this model that it needs some sort of lubricant in the corn for the feed wheel. It was burning out the gearboxes on the feed wheel. My father ran out of corn and he got some corn from the local feed mill. It had a little lubricant in it and it worked great. I'm thinking of putting graphite it the corn for lubrication. It may have less drag on the motor.

What do your children think of your corn stove?

Karen: Usually when the kids come home they gather in the living room where it is warm. They like the heat and the look of the fire as it is running.

Bob: When we first bought the stove in November 2003 they thought we were nuts. They thought we were throwing our money away. We feel like we are pioneers. Now people are calling us asking questions. My son thought it was such a good idea that he put a corn furnace in his home. He is very happy with it. My other son is installing a corn/pellet stove in his home. One of my sisters has put two pellet stoves in her home. My oldest sister has put a corn stove in their garage where they spend most of their time.

What advice would you give someone looking into a corn stove?

Bob: I would recommend a Bixby and an open floor plan. It's efficient, reduces your heating bills, and looks nice.

Do you recommend corn stoves to your family and friends?

Absolutely!!!

I believe in the forest, and in the meadow, and in the night in which the corn grows.— Henry David Throeau

Gary Scott

Location: Marion, IA (suburban)
Square feet heated by corn stove: 2100
Date corn stove purchased: October 2005
Corn storage: 4' cube bin

How was your home heated as a child?

We had a coal furnace. A lot of this reminds me of what my dad had to do. He had to shovel coal into a hopper. It had an auger from the hopper to the furnace. Then periodically he had to shut it down and remove the clinker from the furnace. I remember very well. It was a very hot heat.

Why do you choose to burn corn for heat?

We have a gas furnace, so I wanted to do something different than that, and plus I didn't want the hassle of running a gas line out there. We looked at wood, but wood is messy, when you have a wood fire, it gets real hot and simmers way down, you have to stoke it again. Plus having to have a woodpile and cutting the wood yourself didn't really appeal to me too much. Safety was another reason. I like the renewable fuel, I just really like that. And with my in-laws being farmers, it just made a lot of sense to look to that. So that's really why we were interested in corn over something else.

What sort of research did you do before purchasing the corn stove?

My brother-in-law is a farmer in DeWitte. A couple of years ago he and I were talking about it, and that was the first time I had heard of anything about corn stoves. When I saw Ed's commercial I thought that we should be looking at corn stoves. My wife and I looked at a couple places here in town, and then knowing that Ed was down by Iowa City, we drove down one Saturday to see what he had. We spent quite a bit of time, 2

or 3 hours, at Ed's place, talking to Ed and talking to some of the different customers he had there, too. At that time we were just fishing, getting as much information on the stoves as possible. Then we looked around here a little more and tossed around different models, whether we wanted to go with corn or pellet, and decided we liked the corn the best, and we went back to Ed. I was doing research on different stoves on the internet as well.

How was your stove installed?

I installed it myself. I'm not a handyman, but I can work with tools. Mark delivered the stove, the 2 of us brought it in and set it in the spot. He explained how to vent the exhaust and probably within a couple of hours I had everything in place. I decided to vent it straight out just to see how that worked, and I haven't had any problems with it so far.

How did the temperature of your house during winter compare before and after you began heating with corn?

Normally we're aware and we try to keep the costs down as much as possible. Before, we heated with gas, on a programmable thermostat, it was 65 during the day while we were gone, and in the evening we brought it up to 68 or 70 degrees. Typically we kept it between 80 and 85 degrees last winter. If it was 85 in there, it was typically 10 degrees cooler in the living area, and 10 degrees cooler in the bedroom.

Do you have any accessories with your stove?

I did buy a thermostat for it and also I ended up buying a UPS (uninterruptible power supply) system for it and I plug the stove into that. We had power out one day and the UPS kicked in and the stove kept running, so it was a good investment.

How safe do you perceive your corn stove?

I feel very comfortable with it. If we're going to be gone for a day, we don't have any trouble leaving it running. We just make sure the hopper is full. With a wood stove we wouldn't do that. There are a lot of safety features and sensors in there. If the fire gets hot it shuts down, if the fuel gets low it shuts down.

How do you ignite your stove?

What Ed told me to do was take a cup of pellets, dump it in the firebox, take the starter gel and pour a little on the top. I'd light it with one of those propane lighters, and close the door. I would say it takes 10-15 minutes before you have a good fire and it starts dropping the corn.

Describe stove maintenance and upkeep.

On a daily basis, first thing in the morning I'd make sure the hopper was full. Then at night before I'd go to bed I'd fill it again. That doesn't take 5 minutes. About every day and a half I'd have to drop the clinker. Once in awhile if the fire went out I would do a real thorough cleaning inside. I'd take the shop-vac to it and clean it out real good. I didn't have to empty the ash box as often as I thought I would, maybe once a week. The glass on it gets residue on it and I like to clean that off. The maintenance, I tell you, is minimal.

There was a time when we were going to be gone for a week and my daughter and her fiancé stayed at our house. The night before we left I spent 10-15 minutes with them showing them what to do with the stove. They didn't have any problems with it; they kept the fire going. I think they enjoyed it. It almost makes me wish for winter so I can get the fire going…almost.

Were there any challenges adjusting to your corn stove?

It took me awhile to figure out how to drop the clinker so you don't lose the fire. Once I figured that out, for the most part it's pretty easy, it takes 5 minutes. If you don't catch it in time and the clinker gets too full then you have to shut it down, drop the clinker and restart the fire, and that takes a little longer to do. I was getting pretty good at it. If I caught it every 36 hours I could drop it without starting the fire over again.

Do the benefits of owning a corn stove outweigh the extra work involved?

Absolutely. I enjoy doing it, I enjoy working with it, I enjoy the heat that it puts out. It's an amazing heat. It's such an even heat. With wood it gets so hot and then it dies down. With this it's such an even heat. I really do talk it up to my friends and any chance I get I have them over to have them look at it. It's not for everybody, but it works well here.

Has the corn stove changed how you spend your time at home?

Yes, I found that I was reading out there and not watching television. The problem is that I sit down with a book and it's nice and warm and within 5 minutes I'm probably sleeping, but at least I'm not sleeping in front of the television.

What's burning with ...

Willard Huedepohl

Location: Williamsburg, Iowa (rural)
Number of winters with corn stove: 4
Number of corn stoves: 2
Square feet heated by each stove: 900
Corn or pellet: Corn

Tell me about your corn stove.

It's a Harman stove from Pennsylvania. You pour the corn in the hopper in back and it can hold 70 lbs. When it self-ignites, from the time it starts until the time the fires comes up is about 4 minutes. It's got a fire pot with a stirrer in it that runs at all times. It'll run for over 24 hours before it needs to be refilled.

When did you first encounter the idea of burning corn for heat?

I usually go to farm shows, and several years ago they started selling corn stoves there. I was seeing them for 2 years and the 2nd year I got interested and started really looking hard at what I wanted.

How did you heat your home before you owned a corn stove?

I live out in the country and heated with gas before I bought my corn stoves.

Describe the temperature of your house before and after installing the corn stove.

I keep it around 70-72 degrees in the wintertime now and I kept it at 68 before I had the corn stove. In fact the last year before I got it I had it turned down to 65 degrees.

What was the deciding factor in buying a corn stove?

Heating my house, the price of natural gas was going up. Sitting in a 65 degree house is cold.

Why is corn a better choice for you than natural gas or wood?

Wood is not a cheap thing by the time you cut it and split it. Corn is easy to store, handle and everything else. This stove would burn pellets, and I would like to try gluten pellets if we could get some in. Corncob pellets I don't think would burn as hot as kernels do.

How many people do you know who also have corn stoves?

Quite a few of them: friends and neighbors, my cousin.

What is the biggest benefit to burning corn?

I've almost cut my energy bill in half. Last year this stove upstairs was down for a month. It cost me $100 to heat it with gas for that month.

How do you acquire and store corn?

We rent our ground out and I buy corn from one of our renters. I have a gravity wagon out in the machine shed that I store it in. I fill five gallon buckets and bring about 10 of them in at a time to the garage. The corn has been around 14% moisture, and it needs to be 13% or less, so I started buying corn from the elevator this spring and it worked much better.

How much time did you spend on average hauling corn and maintaining your stoves per week last winter?

This stove doesn't self-maintain like a furnace. You've got to clean the ash out every few days or week depending on how cold it is. It takes a little more work, but it's well worth it. I'm keeping it 7 degrees higher than normal.

Describe any problems you've had with your stoves.

The last two years I've burned out a motor on my exhaust fan. We think now it may have been that my corn was a little too wet, and the fan was blowing too hard. The fan was under warranty and was replaced.

What does your extended family think of your corn stoves?

I told my mom about them and she said that it was good, warm heat. She's 94—she went through the Depression and they burned corn to keep on living back then. Not too many people can say that.

How safe do you perceive your corn stoves to be?

It's hot to the touch on the top and sides, but I have heat shields. The stove is UL approved. It's totally enclosed and nothing can come out of it. The door won't come open because you lock it and it won't start if you don't lock it. It's vacuum operated so if something goes wrong the fire will go out. The fire can't even go out the venting.

What was you're biggest surprise upon heating with corn?

They always said I have to clean it out more often than I do.

What other forms of biomass do you think could be burned as fuel?

I burn ethanol at all times in my truck. I know soybeans don't work in the stove; I tried them.

What's burning with ...

Iowa State Bank and Trust Cindy Mays, West Liberty Branch President & Dan Black, Property Management

Location: West Liberty, Iowa
Year of corn stove installation: 2005,
Heated square footage: 5200 sq. feet

What caused Iowa State Bank and Trust to install a corn stove?

Dan: The architects wanted to design a building that incorporated features that made sense and made a connection to West Liberty. So the stove was just an extension of that whole kind of process and plus the energy conscious part of the thing, with the geothermal. The original design from the architects came back with a gas [fireplace] insert. We instantly realized this was pretty silly because we had a geothermal system in the building. We were going to run a gas line in just to run this fireplace insert, which just struck me as absurd. I made the suggestion that we go this route and the architect really jumped on it. It was really well accepted.

How does it feel to be part of a business with such an open attitude towards change?

Dan: It's really nice that the upper management would consider a corn burner like this. I'm very glad to work for a company that would buy into something that's a little out of the mainstream. I'm really glad they did it and it's been fun.

Cindy: It really feels good for me to be in a small farming community and to proudly be able to say we have a corn-burning stove. For me that makes it a really exciting aspect of this office.

the feel-good heat

How do you view the environmental aspects of burning corn?

Dan: I think this green architecture and engineering is absolutely the wave of the future and I think you're going to see all kinds of people doing this. On the flip side of it, it just has to be. This whole oil thing—we just can't continue to do this.

Where does the bank get its corn?

Cindy: We have farmers in this area with a corn cleaner, and they provide us corn.

How many bushels did you burn per day last winter?

Cindy: We don't even go through a bushel a day, because we also run the geothermal. We shut it down at night, turn it on in the morning, and run it on low during the day. I'll tell you what, it spits out a lot of heat. It's such a nice clean, comfortable heat, and it doesn't smell.

Describe any problems you've had with your stove.

Cindy: One small problem was that you have to have clean corn.

Dan: We had been buying some corn from the local elevator. It had a lot of cracked corn in it and would jam the stove.

Describe customer reaction to the corn stove.

Cindy: It's been very well received. People come into the bank to look because they're curious, or because they are interested in buying one for their house. We've had a few people ask if the corn pops.

Has the corn stove changed where people spend time in the bank?

Cindy: I've had some meetings here, and we don't meet in the conference room; we meet right out here in front of the stove. And it's just a wonderful atmosphere to bring people into and have the corn burner going. It's a win-win. You're not going to hear me say anything bad about it. I think it's just great.

Advice from corn and pellet stove installer and repairman, Mark Hartstack, on selecting and locating a stove for your home.

•Think about your lifestyle. Do you like to tinker with things? Or do you want things to work without much effort? There are a wide variety of stoves on the market; pick one that matches your lifestyle.

•Consider your space. How many square feet do you want to heat? How are your rooms laid out in your house? Corn and pellet stoves heat by convection, so picture the air flowing through your house. Will it travel freely or will it be impaired by walls and doorways? Open floor plans are most conducive to convective air flow.

•Heat where you live. Think about where you spend your time in your home. Most people like warm living rooms and kitchens, but cooler bedrooms. Place your stove so the heat is concentrated where you spend the most time.

•Pat yourself on the back. Using a corn or pellet stove benefits your pocketbook, but also the environment, makes us less dependant on foreign oil, and supports the local economy.

•Don't be fooled by BTUs. The heat output of stoves and furnaces is reported in British Thermal Units, or BTUs per hour. Most gas furnaces have high BTUs because they heat all the air in the house and have to do it quickly. A corn stove heats the air constantly, producing an even heat, and thus needs to produce fewer BTUs.

•Maximize the "wow factor." Corn stoves are a wonderful conversation topic. Put your stove where others can see it - where it can be a focal point in your house.

•Think about fuel storage. How far do you want to carry the corn? Most stoves burn a bushel a day (two five gallon buckets). Think of yourself trudging through the snow or up two flights of stairs, and store your corn as close to your stove as possible. A little planning can save many a footstep. Folks build all sorts of things to store their corn. Be creative.

•Cleaning up. All stoves require cleaning and maintenance. Spilled ash is easier to clean from a tiled floor than carpet. Clinkers are biodegradable so toss them in with the compost or garden.

•Go green and save some green. Go ahead and figure the savings in your heating bills. Tell your friends about it, they'll be jealous. It is not uncommon for stoves to pay for themselves in energy savings within 2-3 years.

What's burning with ...

Dave Jackson

Location: North English, IA (rural)
Area heated by corn stove: 2100 square feet
Number of winters heating with corn: 5

How did you heat your home before you owned a corn stove?

I used LP gas. This is now my fourth season heating with corn.

Why do you choose to burn corn rather than natural gas? Or wood?

LP gas is dependable, but the costs kept going up. It's time we all think about becoming less dependent on fossil fuels. I asked the propane company to pick up that unsightly tank from the yard. That was four years ago.

What were the deciding factors in buying a corn stove?

Initially, it was a tough decision to purchase a corn stove, especially as an alternative to heating with gas. I also wanted to do something to get off dependence on conventional fuels, but really didn't think it was practical, or cost effective. Boy was I wrong! After three full heating seasons with the Bixby corn stove as the sole source of heat, I am fully confident the Bixby 110 will continue to meet my heating needs. I had also heard about the quality of heat that comes from corn, but underestimated the special warmth that it creates.

There's a number of reasons that investing in a Bixby corn stove makes perfect sense. Among those would have to be the technology behind the product. And the technology doesn't stop with the on-board computer, the easy diagnostics, or the improved ash removal. The oxygen concentrator ensures a smooth, efficient burn, so that you get the most for your money whether you use corn, wood pellets or biomass pellets. It burns at 99.7% efficiency. Very little heat leaves the house through the exhaust vent.

Describe how your corn stove works.

The Bixby has an automatic start. A panel much like a microwave oven's features an "On" and "Off," as well as heat settings. The control center is supported by an on-board computer that regulates supply and exhaust air, fuel feed rate, and the ash dump cycle. An igniter lights the corn initially, and concentrated oxygen flows into the firepot. A rotating wheel  carries a few kernels of corn or pellets and drops them into the fire pot approximately every 25 seconds. About every twelve hours, the stove goes through an ash dumping cycle and drops an ash wafer about the size of a large chocolate chip cookie into the ash drawer. The ash is dumped once a week. This means the corn is burning nearly 100%, with little ash being produced. This also means more heat is being produced for the house.

What square footage of your home is heated by your corn stove?

The first winter, 2003, I heated a 2,100 square foot house with a Bixby Model 100, the first generation of the Bixby Corn Stoves. In 2005, I switched over to the Model 110 upgrade, which looks exactly the same from the outside. Whatever the Bixby engineers did to the internal operation is truly an amazing feat. The marriage of low-tech fuel and high-tech solutions has finally arrived.

How do you acquire and store corn?

I can purchase corn from the dealer where I bought the stove, or from a local farmer. I can pick corn up on the way home from work, which minimizes additional fuel used to transport the corn. An 18-gallon plastic storage container full of corn is kept by the stove at all times. I keep the operation fairly low-  tech, placing five to ten of these hard rubber containers in my pick-up once every two or three weeks, when I go on a "corn run." The rest are kept in the storeroom until needed. For additional outside storage, I use two 60 gallon stock tanks, which I set in the pickup bed, and pull under at the auger to load. These are good to keep enough corn stored for back-up in the event of poor driving conditions.

How many bushels did you burn per season?

For the last three full winters, I used between 100 and 125 bushels of corn each season to heat the house for the entire winter. The stove runs from October to early April, and the cost of corn has been between $200 and $250 for the heating season. That's darn good for an Iowa winter! It averages out to a little over a half bushel of corn a day, about a five gallon bucket.

How challenging is maintaining your stove?

This in an easy-to-operate, low maintenance, low-upkeep stove. In general, corn stoves require more cleaning and maintenance than a gas furnace, due to the ash created by burning a solid fuel. I clean the stove on a once-a-week schedule, shutting it off and letting it cool down prior to cleaning. The firebox, burn pot, and mechanical parts get cleaned with a Shop Vac and a special round wire brush that fits into the burn pot. This takes about 10-15 minutes, but is essential to keeping the stove running efficiently. This is much easier than the amount of work involved with heating with wood. And you get used to the routine, and taking pride in keeping the stove operating at peak efficiency.

How safe do you perceive your corn stove?

One key factor in my decision to buy a Bixby is the product safety. The stove exterior is warm, not hot to the touch, when the unit is in full operation. The blower technology keeps the heat flowing out of the unit, along with the twelve heat exchanger tubes. All this combines to create a product that can be installed in close tolerance (3" from walls on the side) and provides optimal air circulation.

The 3" exhaust pipe on the outside is warm, but not so hot that I can't hold my hands around it for several seconds. A 5" intake pipe surrounds the exhaust pipe; the "pipe within a pipe" intake / exhaust flue system is cool to the touch when the unit is operational, and is easy to install.

Overall, my advice is that a corn stove is not for everyone. You can't simply turn on the thermostat and walk away from it for weeks and months on end, like most people do with their gas furnace. However, with a minimal amount of labor and care for the corn stove, it becomes a great source of pride and will create a "feel-good" heat for many years. You can view a complete account of Dave's experiences with the Bixby corn stove, as well as additional photos like the ones in his interview, at: http://www.hinkletown.com/bixby.html

Another way that biomass energy is truly a feel-good heat. Each year Century Farm Harvest Heat hosts a corn maze as a local fundraiser, providing thousands of dollars for area groups such as the local Big Brother/Big Sister's program. The corn maze (in October the maze converts into the Field of Screams) is a fun way to be immersed in a field of fuel. Events such as these also encourage local economies to increase biomass education by immersion. As the future of biomass develops tours will continue with other biomass resources.

Jim Shepherd

Location: Muscatine, IA (rural)
Corn or pellet: corn
Number of winters with a corn stove: 2
Number of corn stoves: 2 (one furnace, one stove)
Square feet heated by each stove: 2300+

When did you first encounter the idea of burning corn for heat?

I had never heard of corn heat, but I had used wood heat in the past quite a bit and had a lot of experience with that. I was really interested in an alternative type of heat so I started looking into corn a little bit and I was just fascinated by it. I decided I wanted a corn furnace for my new log home, because that was going to be my primary source of heat. I was going to put in a standard furnace, but that was going to be my backup. We put a freestanding corn stove in my other house, where we lived during construction of the log home, because my first LP bill after the price increase was $800 for less than half a tank. We did use some LP but we still never needed the tank filled again, so it must have been doing a good job. I'm still running on the same tank that we initially had. We needed both houses all winter. We weren't able to officially move in to the log home until summer 2006. But we had to keep the log home warm so I could work on it.

You innovatively designed the setup of your corn and LP furnaces. Describe this process.

What I wanted to do was introduce the corn furnace into the cold air return into the standard furnace and draft it right through. The main thing I was interested in was the temperature of the electronic component in the corn furnace, because if it wasn't getting enough draft from the regular furnace, the temperature would go up dangerously high. It was all theory. I monitored the temperature in a controlled study so I knew exactly where it ran all by itself, temperature-wise. So then, I set it up so

it blew into the standard furnace and I had that blower running all the time. I put a probe very close to where that brain on the corn furnace was—I wanted to make sure that it wasn't running any higher than it was with just the corn burner running. What I found was I was actually able to pull the temperature down lower than where the standard unit ran. Because of that it meant that I wasn't hurting the corn furnace I wasn't hurting the other furnace and everybody was happy, especially me.

Eventually, the way I have my corn furnace set up is I don't even use the blower on my corn furnace. I'm using the blower all the time from my LP furnace. It's incorporated into the whole heating system, the way they normally set up furnaces. I'm able to draft my corn furnace into that other system and it draws enough air that it keeps my corn furnace cool and normal. I literally heated through the LP furnace all winter long.

Why do you choose to burn corn rather than wood in your new log home?

When I started looking into corn, it fascinated me because it had all the pros that wood didn't have. There are serious issues with wood heat that most people—even your insurance companies—don't like. I don't want a fireplace, I want something that works. A fireplace is dirtier than a corn burner. You can say what you want but a fireplace is not going to be able to do a complete heat job, I don't think.

How do you acquire and store corn?

The corn is in the bins already stored on the premises. I lease out my bins and I called the guy and asked him if I could buy grain from him and he said as long as I weigh it. We got a gravity wagon—there seems to be a few of those around—and are able to screen the corn as it comes out of the wagon and store it in 5 gallon buckets that are carried to both units. We were

gravity wagon

running 15% moisture corn, which is a little high, but it made it. The furnace had a little bit of trouble with the moisture if I had it set too high.

I'd have gone through three tanks in a normal winter. Well, it would've cost me, to heat that other house, at least $2500-3500 for the rest of last winter. We were able to basically heat both houses from December on, with about $400 worth of corn.

Describe routine maintenance on your corn furnace and stove.

The corn furnace in the cabin is not nearly as user friendly as the stove, which is in the other house. The unit in the house is really neat—it's easy to operate, it's very easy to clean, so it makes it real easy to run. The furnace is not as easy to operate, is not as easy to run and is way harder to clean. It's not as easy to clean because basically the clinker has got to come out—as hard as I was running it, I had to clean it almost every day, which meant I had to shut it down daily. Next year I'm going to make the furnace run like the stove—I'm going to make the box so I can drop the clinker out. I'm betting I'm still going to have to shut it down, but it's going to be a whole lot easier to clean that clinker out of there.

What was you're biggest surprise upon heating with your stove?

One of the big things that log homes have got going for them is the thermal mass —once you get them warm, they hold it. On the other hand when they're cold like when we first got the corn furnace lit—I really thought the next morning it was going to be at 50 degrees and everybody was going to be happy. Wrong. The next morning the thermostat upstairs was at about 35 degrees. Within a month we had it up to 60 or 65 degrees upstairs, which is as high as I wanted it for working, and we were able to maintain it.

Ken Kemper

Location: Anamosa, IA (rural)
Square footage heated: 1700 feet (home)
Corn or pellet: corn
Number of corn stoves: 2

When did you first encounter the idea of burning corn for heat?

My business partner and I had been looking at ways to heat our building during construction while gas was removed from the site. He'd been online investigating and had heard about corn stoves. Once we started learning and investigating the price of stoves and corn we decided we wanted to give it a try. We bought three stoves; he put one in his house, we put one in the building and I put one in my home which is a farm. This year I'm going to be moving the corn stove from the commercial building into my home and burning corn almost exclusively.

What advice would you give someone considering a corn stove for his or her home?

My word of advice for somebody, especially during the summertime, would be don't wait for the leaves to get off the trees before you start looking because you won't be able to find one. We waited about 2 ½ months to get ours and finally got it around November.

How did you heat your home before you used corn?

I used heating oil, which was my main source of heating. I also had a wood stove as an auxiliary to take the load off the oil.

Did you heat exclusively with corn last winter?

Last year I did use a little bit of wood. On the really cold days, if it was in the lower teens or single digits, I'd burn wood through the night to keep the nip off the south end of the house, and then I'd use just corn for the rest of the day. My regular furnace is in the same room as the corn stove, so it would really never kick on.

How many bushels of corn did you go through last winter?

At home, I was using about $45 worth of corn per month running on low.

Why is burning corn more appealing to you than continuing to burn wood or fuel oil?

As I get older I don't care to be out in the woods cutting and splitting wood. Knowing the effort and danger that goes into going out and splitting wood. It is good exercise, but I need my time for other things. There was also the cost factor; fuel oil has definitely gone up. It would probably be $2000 to heat with oil - it's an old farmhouse. The fact that I can keep my house warmer than I could afford to do with a furnace is appealing.

Where do you get corn, and how do you store it?

I have a neighbor who grows corn and beans and I made arrangements with him to get corn. I buy it at the tipping weight cost, which can be anywhere from 15 to 25 cents cheaper per bushel. Living out in the country, right next to farmers is just another reason why burning corn just makes all that much more sense. I bought a corn wagon—150 bushel—I'll take the wagon down, have my neighbor fill it up, drive it down to the scale, write him a check and park it in the garage.

How safe do you perceive your corn stove?

There are so many things that make it a safer alternative. The corn stove will probably lower my insurance as well. They really look hard at the installation, and the corn stove is a self-contained automatic unit; if the door is open, if power isn't right, it shuts down. If I would have tried to put a wood stove in my living room, I would've

77

had to have everything 3 feet away from it. With these things you can get them right into tight spaces because there's not a lot of radiant heat on the box. You can put your hand right on it. It's much more space-efficient to have this right up in a corner and to be able to have things close to it.

What sort of time requirement did your stove require last winter?

I'd spend maybe about a half hour every weekend when I'd go over and get 4 or 5 bushels and run them right through the cleaner. That is not going to take me as long this year having all the corn on site in the garage. I'll be able to clean enough corn for all week in about 15 minutes.

Describe any problems you've had with your stove.

I have had some times when if I didn't drop the clinker out by about the 2nd day it would stick in there pretty hard and I'd have to take a chisel to it. If you keep it pretty clean, you'll be fine. There are stoves out there now that have agitators, some are totally automatic, this one is not, but I don't mind. Dust is a little bit of an issue. Keeping the things around the stove dusted and pouring the corn in slow enough that you don't create as much dust is important. Maybe if I rigged up a vacuum to my corn cleaner to suck that dust out of there, that would cut a lot of the dust. I'm sure as these things become more common, people will come up with more ways to reduce the dust and other things.

How do visitors react to your corn stove?

Everybody asks me about it. Before I open up the hopper and show them the corn they think it's a wood stove, and then they think it's a pellet stove. I do get a lot of reaction and it's always positive—especially when I tell them what I pay for my heat per month. For somebody who's living in the city and used to totally maintenance-free heat, then a corn stove might not be for them. I consider this quite easy, but it's not maintenance free by any means. I like being involved in that sort of thing. It's not for everybody, but it is for me.

What's burning with ...

Steve and Sonja Moss

Location: Iowa City, IA (Suburban)
Square footage heated by stove: 4000
Number of winters with a corn stove: 2
Corn or pellet: corn

How did you heat your home before you owned a corn stove?

Steve: A natural gas line. We were at $300 per month before we got the stove and we figured we'd be at $500 last year with the price increases. We only hit over $200 one month last year. The corn stove has 5 levels and we ran it at level 3 almost all the time. We turned it down to 1 when we had everyone here at Christmas. You have good control of it; if you turn it down, it goes down, it doesn't burn as much corn and it's not as hot.

What was your first reaction to the idea of burning corn for heat?

Sonja: We'd been talking about corn stoves for a long time, and our friends and family had read all of the articles, so they all knew of them, but no one else had taken the initiative to go look at them and buy one. So we took the lead.

Steve: My father used corn in the 30s for some of their heat. Both my grandparents were farmers and we had corncobs, which we stuck in at the end. I was familiar with using parts of the corn, but I wasn't familiar with using the kernels, and people still have trouble fathoming using the kernels and not the cobs. I read about corn stoves in the newspapers and magazines both.

Has the corn stove changed how you spend your time at home?

Sonja: We never could use this room in the winter because it's not heated below; it's a garage below. And even though we have heat ducts out here, with all the windows it doesn't heat.

Steve: Traditionally this was a great room 3 seasons out of the year. Now it's an even better room in the wintertime because we have an attractive fire. That's what it amounts to. It's such a great heat source. I just find it fun to curl up over here. I went to an auction and bought that couch so I could have a couch right here in front of it.

Do you recommend corn stoves to your friends?

Steve: I've shown each and every one of my neighbors our stove. Anybody who's interested in corn stoves would be welcomed into my home to take a look at mine.

Describe operating and maintaining your stove.

Steve: My mechanical skills are not real solid and operating the stove is pretty much a no brainer—there's just not a whole lot to it. You pour the corn in, light the fire and it burns. It's pretty fail safe. I wish there was a way to keep the glass from getting dirty over time, but that's so easy to wipe down, you just open the door and wipe it down with a dry cloth. But as far as the maintenance, there's really not a lot that you have to do other than taking the clinker out. We dump it in the side yard and the deer come up and eat them.

Sonja: For me, the only drawback to the whole thing—the extra steps to putting the corn in ourselves, I didn't mind any of that at all—but it was the dust. When they delivered it and when we pour it in the hopper. Every day you have to dust it off. Ed said they already have a remedy for the dust, soybean oil.

How do you acquire and store corn?

Steve: I buy corn from Ed just for the convenience of doing it. I keep my corn in one of Ed's cubes in the garage, up on blocks and I put my 5 gallon bucket underneath it. We know we have mice in the garage, but having the corn did not bring any mice into the house. As long as they're careful when they're putting the corn in, it's all contained in the hopper.

Sonja: Periodically some corn spills, especially when they fill the hopper. We try to keep it swept up, but we never noticed any go missing.

How would you improve your corn stove?

Steve: There's some design flaws in this stove. I love the dang thing, but sometimes the clinker doesn't drop like it's supposed to. Why is that? They should've taken care of that in the design phase. There's a whole lot they can do that they haven't done yet. If I had any mechanical aptitude, I'd develop a stove. I think it's wonderful that you can go to your local neighbor and buy your heat for the winter. I personally don't know why every farmer in Iowa doesn't have a corn stove.

I would want a hopper that I could put on a stand, right outside my door, feeding the corn through a chute so it gently tumbles right into my hopper. It's so simple. In the old days they had the coal chutes to get the coal right down into the basement. Corn is a heck of a lot cleaner than coal. It'd make it a lot more functional.

Do the benefits of owning a corn stove outweigh the extra work involved?

Steve: If it takes pouring a 5 gallon bucket of corn in, then so be it. If it takes pouring a paint can full of corn in because you're older and feebler, it's no big deal. It's good exercise for the day. There's really not much to it.

Kathrin Schmidt

*Also in household: Tom Schmidt
(husband)*
Location: Iowa City, IA (urban)

Note: At the time of this interview Kathrin had recently purchased and was in the process of having a corn stove installed.

When did you first encounter the idea of corn stoves?

The first time I heard about it was in the local news. I thought it was fascinating because I had no idea that corn actually could be burned. I was fascinated by the guy in this story, who said he was heating his whole house with corn. I wondered how you could do that, and why it was not more popular. I thought the downside must be very big that people don't gravitate toward it, that there must be a major issue with it. Then I found out that's not necessarily true. The second time I came across the idea was up in Cedar Rapids, Iowa where they had a home show and that was the first time we looked at a corn stove in person.

What process did you go through deciding if a corn stove would work for you?

Last year I was debating a wood stove, but because you have to let the stove cool off in order do remove they daily ashes, it just didn't really appeal to me. Plus the whole stove gets very hot and I didn't like that either, so I just let it go. I can see the advantages of a corn stove, with it continuously burning.

The initial idea was to heat this side of the house a little more. We were not quite sure if a corn stove would look right in this room, so I thought we might switch to a furnace, also because it would put the warm air into the duct work and make it comfortable throughout the whole house. I investigated that, and nobody could really convince me that would be the right solution for this house, so we went back to the stove. In interim times like fall and winter it's easy to turn it on and heat the parts of the house where you live versus the whole house by just turning the stove on. That's very appealing to me.

What is your main reason for wanting the corn stove?

The heat is the main reason. Due to the fact that it burns totally clean, it's attractive to me. The older I get, the more concerned I am with the environment: it's certainly something I want to integrate into my decisions. When corn is a resource right in front of your door and when you can generate something with it, why look further?

Why do you think most people don't have corn stoves?

I think people maybe aren't willing to put in the little amount of time that it needs every day. You do have to remove the clinker, depending on how much you're burning. Plus there might be some dust going around and maybe some people are concerned with having mice because you store the corn close to your home. It's not just turning your thermostat higher or lower, there is a little bit of physical labor involved in it.

Do you have any of these same concerns?

No way. It's just part of life, you have to be engaged. It's not an issue for me. You might have to carry the corn downstairs, but you're going down there anyway, so why go empty-handed? Why not take a bucket with you, you might lose a gram. So it's absolutely not an issue, it's nothing that would keep me away from burning corn.

Do you know anyone who has a corn stove?

Not right now. Every time I mention it to a friend, they say, "What, a corn stove? Do you burn the whole ear?" They've never heard of it.

Have you had any challenges in the process of getting a corn stove?

There are several companies who manufacture hearth pads, but they usually stock only the most common sizes and the color of the tiles are just standard like gray, black, white, and light brown. We needed a corner pad in a small size and this would have been a special order and would haven taken 5-6 weeks for delivery, which was just too long. In addition, distributors warned me that they easily brake in the shipping process and I feared that could potentially delay the installation. After about a week of research, I found a man who would come in and custom build a hearth pad. However, when I went into the store to order tiles I liked, I found out it takes two weeks to get them. But this was still faster than the conventional way.

You grew up in Switzerland; are corn and pellet stoves popular there?

Not at all, they would have to import corn to burn. What they do have is wood chips. My dad heats thousands of square feet with wood. He has a construction business, so when they tear down old buildings he gets called in to run it through a wood chipper. He blows the chips into a space above the heater. At the bottom there is a huge rotating arm that drops the chips into the heater. The heater heats water in a huge tank and the water is pumped to four single-family homes for heat, offices, and four huge construction maintenance buildings.

When people plant corn they are saying, let's stay here. And by their connection to the land, they are connected to one another."—Anne Raver

the feel-good heat

Mary Somerville

Location: Oxford, IA (rural)
Also in household: Kevin
Square footage heated by the corn stove: 1300 square feet
Corn or pellets: corn
Winters with corn stove: 2

How does it feel being a pioneer of the energy world?

I guess it feels really fine. We really wanted to get a corn stove early on when Ed was just starting to get into it. It just made a lot of sense.

How did you heat your home before you owned a corn stove?

We've gone through a lot of eras in this house, on energy. We started with a fuel oil furnace and when that died we started burning wood with a wood heater. Then we started getting older and it was kind of messier and we didn't have the time to do all the harvesting. And we had little kids around the house and we got really lazy and put in a propane furnace which was energy efficient, kind of state of the art for its time. And at that time fuel wasn't really expensive. Then when energy costs were going up and I learned about the technology, a corn stove just made a lot of sense.

How many winter seasons have you had a corn stove?

We got a corn stove from Ed last fall. It was kind of a mild winter, but the little corn stove down there in our sun room was really all we needed for the whole house, both upstairs and downstairs. So we were really impressed right off. During January when we did have a cold spell it just ran pretty much non-stop. We really got into dropping the brick, stoking it up again, keeping the hopper full.

Describe the temperature of your house before and after installing the corn stove?

We keep it quite toasty. When we were doing the propane, we had our thermostat turned down and we were bundled up. Now we're kicking the quilt off at night. It's a lot warmer with the corn stove in most of the house. At times I think about getting a small one for the kitchen area.

What were the deciding factors in buying a corn stove?

Whether or not we could afford it was one, but we knew we'd be saving so that was crossed off the list. We just knew we wanted another source of heat and working with Ed, we knew we'd get a good one. I'd seen his so I knew it worked. There was starting to be more about it in the press.

Describe any environmental aspects of burning corn?

The obvious thing is that it is a renewable energy. It doesn't take us much energy to get it from the producer to our home. It's that whole transport system that we cut out. The efficiency of the corn burner is a plus. You don't have waste that has to be disposed of, other than a small quantity of ash, which you can just set in the flower beds. Negatives, I can't think of any.

How much corn did you burn last season?

When it was really cold we went through a bushel per day. There were times in the spring when we might start it up and run it for a couple hours just to take the chill off. We filled and emptied a big, old hopper wagon for the winter, which was $400 worth of corn. That was really good, because other years with propane we might have spent as much as a couple thousand dollars. We will recover in one year what we paid for our stove. This coming winter it's really going to dawn on us how much we're going to save. We'll still have our propane at least partially filled, just for a backup. It'll be fun to see how many years until we empty it.

How much time did you spend on average hauling corn and maintaining your stove per week last winter?

Compared to wood heat it's hardly anything. It couldn't be more than a half hour per week. It's a little more work than going over to adjust the thermostat, but it isn't a lot of work. Compared to other alternatives, there's just no comparison. With wood you have to go out and split it and stack it, and bring it in. The ash accumulates faster, it's dirtier.

Describe any problems you've had with your stove?

We went through some real learning. I think the manual is made by people that make the stove, not the people that run the stove. I'd call up Ed and he'd give me tips, and by halfway through the winter we were pretty swift at operating it and running it. The biggest challenge was learning about dropping the brick, the timing of that. If you let it go too long you really had a mess. Some of that was just experience and we made some mistakes. The fact of the matter is that you learn about the routine and how to do it.

What advice would you give someone considering a corn stove for his or her home?

Try to deal with the storage issue. First of all people are pretty naive about bushels of corn and how much space a bushel takes up. The average recycling bin you see along the street is about a bushel. The advice I'd like to give to people is the volume of corn storage space they really should have available if they want to have 2 weeks of corn on hand. Also the closer you have storage to where you have the stove, the better.

Other advice would be to get a good source for your fuel. Make sure you have a farmer that knows all about moisture content.

I'm not sure there's enough information out there about where to locate the stove in your home. We weren't aware of some of the restrictions about not having the vent near a window and some of the other specs and codes.

What sort of reaction do visitors have to your corn stove?

People that would come to visit us would always be surprised. They'd go "Oh that's a corn stove?!" I don't know what they thought; it was going to be shaped like a corn cob pipe? They'd look at it and they'd feel the  heat and they'd go "Wow, this is really something. Well, where's the corn at?" I think some people thought we were burning ground up corn cobs, some people thought maybe a whole ear of corn like a log.

What does your family think of your corn stove?

The kids really appreciate having that source of heat, standing by it and warming up. Our grand kids really love it too. Everybody kind of appreciates having it in the house. With the grand kids we're especially happy with how safe it is, if they would back into it or touch it, it wouldn't burn them. That was always a concern when we had the old wood-burning stove.

Has the corn stove changed how or where your family spends its time?

It kind of pulled us into the sun room more, it pulled us out to where it was because it's just nice to have a flame. It kind of affected our lifestyle, we spent less time in front of the TV and more time in front of the fire. We saved some money and had some good heat.

How safe do you perceive your corn stove?

It's not like you're messing with gas valves. It's all so safe. Good engineering and I'm sure they'll just get better, even more user friendly.

What is your reaction to the George Washington Carver quote?

I wholeheartedly agree with George Washington Carver, probably for lots of reasons. As far as our material needs and foods, that was all met on the farm as a child. What also strikes me about that quote is that I've become kind of a student of Native American spirituality. They just have a whole different attitude toward the gifts of the Earth, that they were put here for our use. They've learned lots of creative ways to use them, for their own medicine and sustenance and showed a lot of respect too, for those gifts. So all those things for me all come together and I just am in agreement with George and Ed on those things.

The day of fortune is like a harvest day, We must be busy when the corn is ripe.
—Torquato Tasso

Zac Wedemeyer

Location: Iowa City, IA (urban)
Other members of household:
Elesa, wife; Iris & Ani, daughters
Number of winters with
corn stove: 2
Square footage of home: 1700
Corn or pellets: corn

What initially made corn stoves appealing to you?

When Elesa and I got married two years ago after courting for about three months, we had hashed out a lot of our life philosophies and what our ideal life parameters were. One was becoming as self-sufficient as we could, like generating electricity, using renewable fuels and all that stuff.

When did you first hear about corn stoves and what was your reaction?

We didn't know about corn kernels as a fuel. So many people say, "Corn stove, oh that burns corn cobs, right?" At the Earth Expo last year, we were just going around and Elesa bumped into Ed and said, "Give me your spiel, sell me." The idea, when Ed really started talking about it was almost a no brainer. It really was just lucky. It will be able to pay us back.

What influenced your ultimate decision to burn corn instead of wood or natural gas?

The idea that the fuel is actually good fuel. We were planning on getting a wood insert for the fireplace. I think there are advantages to wood, but not practical advantages. I think corn is really more convenient and cleaner. There's a lot of work that goes into getting natural gas, and it's done in a way that I don't think is good for the earth. Corn farming is a little bit better and it's grown three miles away.

Was the corn stove your primary source of heat last winter?

This house is really not very tight and it's expensive to heat, even though it's a small house. The corn stove would heat the living room beautifully and most of the downstairs pretty well. Upstairs was a little more difficult, but it was ok because on all but the coldest nights our furnace wouldn't run. Our bedrooms would be pretty cool. The baby's room would be cool, but she sleeps better that way. It was not what I would call the primary source of heat, but a large companion. What we found out was that most average heating bills went up 35% maybe, and ours went down about 5%, so I think it was pretty significant.

What do you consider the environmental advantages to burning corn?

Burning corn doesn't add to the carbon cycle because it's plant material and the carbon is already loose in the environment anyway, whereas burning fossil fuel that has been stored away indefinitely puts carbon back into the atmosphere. With fossil fuel, it has to be dug up from the ground, which is harmful to the environment and dangerous. Then it has to be shipped tremendous distances using more fossil fuel and resources. With corn, there are still some things that I'm concerned about, I just think that farming it 3 miles out of town and trucking it into town is so much safer than fossil fuel burning.

How much corn did you go through?

On the coldest days I think we burned 15-20 gallons (1.5-2 bushels). Most of the 20-30 degree cold days we burned 10-15 gallons (1-1.5 bushels) per day. For some people, and for me at first, it was hard to accept the idea of burning corn kernels as not being a waste of corn. We burn 15 gallons of corn a day, which seems like a lot. I don't know how many cubic feet of gas you'd burn. It makes more visible the resources that go

into heating, but I don't think it's out of line with other methods that are used. So it was fairly easy to wrap my head around that.

How did you adjust to the first couple of months of using your stove?
Even though it wasn't super involved, I did have to have some skill and develop some skill to keep the stove going. First of all, there was a process of learning how to build the fire so it was a good fire, a balanced fire. We were new parents as well, so a lot of times in the morning Elesa would go off to work, Iris would be asleep and I'd have a very limited time to get done the things I needed to do. Many mornings I used all that time screwing with the stove, keeping it going or getting it going. But it was really satisfying when it was going, it was a real accomplishment to think that we were having to put effort and thought into keeping our house warm, which people don't usually have to do.

> I love to study the many things that grow below the corn stalks and bring them back to the studio to study the color. If one could only catch that true color of nature—the very thought of it drives me mad.
> —Andrew Wyeth

Darren and Becky West

Location: Riverside, IA (rural)
Other household members: Bryce, Drew and Kayla
Corn or pellets: corn
Number of winters with a corn stove: 3
Square footage heated: 2100

Describe the temperature of your house before and after installing the corn stove?

I use the convection heat to draw the air up and heat the upstairs. It does fairly well. The downstairs, where we keep the stove, is toasty; a lot warmer than it's ever been. With the corn stove it stays between 65 and 68 upstairs, depending on how cold it is out. We keep it set at level 6 out of 8. If we leave, we bump it down a little bit so we don't run out of corn.

How did you heat your home before you owned a corn stove?

Propane. And we prefer not to use it. We do make sure to always have some propane just in case we would need it.

How do you acquire and store corn?

It's interesting, the first year we got it from Ed. The next year we got some from the coop. Then a neighbor took some from his field and put it in his gravity wagon and put it in our shed. We bring it in with bushel tubs and we sift through it so there's no corncobs and stuff. We're very picky what we put in there.

How fast did you go through corn?

It depended on how cold it is. I would say if you fill it up it'd last a day. It'll go 24 hours or more if you fill it full.

What type of work did maintaining your stove require last winter?

It's less work than a wood stove. Storing corn is easy. Almost every other day to every day we would take the clinker out and dump the pan outside, which took only a few minutes. I'd shut it down, vacuum, and wipe off the glass once a week, which would take about an hour.

What do your children think of your corn stove?

They'll go and stand in front of the heat when it's blowing, when they come inside from the cold. They like to sift through the corn before we dump it in. They really enjoy playing in the corn and helping dump it in the hopper.

What was your biggest surprise heating with your stove?

I was surprised that there wasn't more of a forced air heat; that it was a slow steady heat and it still kept the whole house relatively warm. And it's not messy. I've always had this idea that corn would be a big mess and, except when the kids would get in it, it never was.

Have you had any maintenance trouble?

When we got it in December of 2004 it didn't work for the first few months. It would run for two weeks and then it would shut down again. We finally got it running in January or February. We dinked around, put a new motor and igniter wire in it. This past winter the tech guy came down and changed the motor again, and all the wires, and reset the settings. The tubes in the back clog up and aren't able to be cleaned out. Currently we have a frayed heat seal that will need to be replaced.

Do you recommend corn stoves to your family and friends?

We have, even though it didn't work at first, we still did. Just make sure it burns. We had Thanksgiving down here and Darren's family just loved it. All the men looked at it and then never left the downstairs where it was nice and toasty.

What is the best reason to burn biomass?

You don't have to spend as much on propane every year. It's good for helping farmers out too. You're using what you're producing on the land. Even though we're not farmers, it is still a good thing. It's a win-win for everybody.

Harvest Heat and biomass heating is no longer a fad. Once a month, twelve months a year, people call in to ask questions, listen and find out what's happening with biomass and stoves during the "Expert Hour" show featuring Harvest Heat on WMT AM600 out of Cedar Rapids, Iowa.

Picture above are Mike Ott with BIOWA, Mary Audia and Ed Williams with Harvest Heat.

Doug Yansky Auto Repair
Doug Yansky

Location: Iowa City, IA (suburban)
Heats with used motor oil & corn stoves
Years with a corn stove: 4
Number of units: 2 corn stoves, 1 corn furnace
Total cost of heating last winter: $400
Corn or pellets: corn

What square footage of your shop is heated by your corn stove?

10,00 square feet. It does okay until it gets around zero and the wind is blowing. My main source of heat is used motor oil; the corn is a back-up. It's a little safer than the used oil.

How warm do you keep your shop?

Warm enough so you can work with your gloves off, a little warmer in the office. My daughter works in the office and she likes it a little warmer so we have the corn stove blowing in there.

Why do you choose to burn corn rather than natural gas or wood?

I'm into saving money. I burn wood at home. It would be too much work to heat a shop and home with wood. I'm doing it to save money. As soon as gas is cheaper than corn, I'll turn the gas on. Early this last spring 400 gallons of natural gas was $800. A wagon load of corn is $400 for 200 bushel. We burn about a bushel a day. We're saving lots of money.

How do you acquire and store corn?

I own several farms around here. We store it straight from the field into a gravity wagon.

What advice would you give someone looking at a corn stove?

You want good, solid kernels because the stove won't burn powder. Small pieces will clog the chute. I wouldn't buy some weird off-the-wall brand. I'd buy something that's been out for a while that you can get parts and service for.

How much time did you spend on average hauling corn and maintaining your stove per week or month last winter?

10-15 minutes per day average. You dump the clinker once every few days. Every once in awhile you have to shut it down and take a vacuum and clean it out like a wood stove.

Have you experienced any problems with your stove?

Yeah, but my brother's an electrical engineer. And the mechanical part I can usually figure out. It's like troubleshooting cars.

What sort of reaction do you get from customers?

A lot of people ask what we're doing with the corn in here. Most people are pretty fascinated by it when they see it.

What do your kids think of your corn stove?

My kids have grown up with it, they're used to it. One of their chores is to fill all the corn.

How safe do you perceive your corn stove?

Pretty safe. It burns pretty cool; you can grab the pipe going out. I don't think it puts out any CO_2. You can go outside and it smells like it's burning popcorn. Even if you breathed it in, it wouldn't have enough CO content to really hurt anyone I wouldn't think.

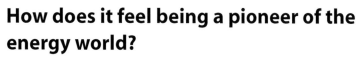

David Zollo

Location: Iowa City (rural)
Other members of household: Beth Oxier, wife; Rocco, son (see right)
Corn or biomass: Corn
Number of seasons with corn stove: 2
Number of corn stoves: 2
Square feet heated by stove: 3000

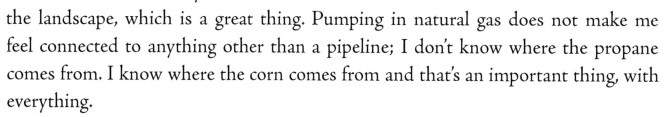

How does it feel being a pioneer of the energy world?

It's awesome. It makes you feel connected to the landscape, which is a great thing. Pumping in natural gas does not make me feel connected to anything other than a pipeline; I don't know where the propane comes from. I know where the corn comes from and that's an important thing, with everything.

When did you first encounter the idea of burning corn for heat?

I had a friend who had a corn stove, and I read a couple articles, one in a national publication and one in the local paper. I'd already been exploring the possibility of getting one and then these articles talked about heating your home for $40 per month. We were just getting ready to move out into this huge house, and that's what kind of sealed it for us.

Why is burning corn a good choice for your family?

I made a conscious choice when I moved back from Nashville to do things a certain way and to live life a certain way. Our philosophy involves living in a way where we're conserving as much as possible, and we're contributing to the local economy. There are a lot of things you can do to make a small, local—which is where you start—contribution to this bigger idea of conservation.

How well do your corn stoves heat your home?

In the dead of winter we heated the whole home without running the furnace at all, with those two corn stoves. Some of the outlying rooms could get not even chilly, just a tad brisk. The living quarters, the common spaces and the bedrooms are all plenty warm.

How do you acquire and store corn?

I buy corn directly now from a friend of mine who farms to feed his livestock. The only problem we had last year was getting enough corn, because we don't have a good storage container. But we've got that problem taken care of now. We got a bulk bin from a farmer friend, it's about a hundred-bushel bulk bin, so we should be set.

How have friends and family reacted to your corn stove?

Everybody that I know, my friends and family, are proponents of this kind of thing. My parents were hard core radical hippies, so nothing I do surprises them. They think it's great.

How did your dog react to the stove?

Babe is an old Boxer so her joints tend to be a little sore. She loves the corn stove—she plops down right in front of it.

How much time did you spend on average hauling corn and maintaining your stove last winter?

Not much. I'd say 10-15 minutes per day filling it and cleaning it. Daily, you just have to empty the clinker, and then you have to pull this little rod a few times to clean the finer dust out. It's really negligible when I think about how much of my day I waste doing stupid stuff; it's a small price to pay.

Has your corn stove been a good investment financially?

I think in the 4 month period we only used about $200 worth of propane. It would've normally been $300 per month to heat this house. That's dryer, stove, oven, water heaters—pretty impressive. It's a win-win proposition.

How many bushels did you burn per day/week?

I couldn't say. We went through more than what they advertised, but we have a big house, and it's a high ceiling house—I think the ceiling is 25′. I would fill it a couple times per day. It would depend greatly on how much time we spend in different parts of the house.

How safe do you perceive your corn stove?

They're safe. We're fortunate that Rocco's a pretty cautious child. I don't know if he was a more aggressive 3-year-old boy if it would've been more of a risk, but he won't go near it. He helps us fill it and will play in the corn. This feels a lot safer to me than a wood stove; you don't have any sparks.

Do you recommend corn stoves to your family and friends?

I've probably sold a half a dozen of them just by word of mouth.

What are the biggest benefits to burning corn?

The biggest benefits are environmental, synergy with the local economy, and then, you know, the savings. If this cost the same amount as heating with natural gas and propane, I would still do this. Because of my friends and people I grew up with who are farmers, especially a year ago when corn was really, really low, devalued, it was under $2 a bushel.

Glen and Ginger Hanson

Location: Iowa City, IA (urban)
Winters with a corn stove: 2
Corn or pellets: corn
Square feet heated by stove: 1500

How did you end up with a corn stove?

Ginger: I was pretty reluctant in the beginning. I was concerned that the maintenance of it would be hard for me. I wanted to be able to operate it myself, to know if I could. But Glen got me to believe in it so much, and reading about it I thought it was really the way we needed to go. We loved the idea of having the fireplace but efficiency-wise, we were losing all the heat up the chimney, so this was a good alternative. But it's been so easy, and the constant heat—I just love that. Instead of getting up in the morning and it being so cold and turning the heat way up—it's always warm.

How warm do you keep the house in the winter?

Glen: It's generally always 80° degrees (F) right here in this room. I would say last year there was one week that we had to have an electric heater upstairs at night, but otherwise, this did it all.

Ginger: And it's an odd house for that because it's not like it's one open space where all the heat can go, there are so many nooks and crannies. We've had to kind of figure out how to get the heat around. A little fan will take it where we want it to go, and of course heat rises. In the bedrooms it's typically an average of 65 degrees, which is good for sleeping.

Glen: Now see, I'm a Sourthern boy. I can't stand it here. The more heat I get, the more I like it. Last year we paid $180 for all the corn we could smoke. And if you

figured on a 6 month heating season, that was $30 per month. My utility bills never exceeded $50 for gas and electric. Actually, the delivery charge for the gas to the house exceeded my consumption bill—and we heat our water and cook on the stove with gas. You become a struttin' fool when you're out there talking about your corn stove.

What did you pay for gas to heat your home before the corn stove?

Glen: I looked up a bill the other day and it was almost $300 in February. Now we pay around $50 for both gas and electric. These motors have to be using quite a bit less than your motor on a typical heater. I could run these overnight on a couple of solar collectors.

Ginger: That's another step. The sun, the wind, what else can we use?

Has the corn stove changed how you spend time at home?

Ginger: Actually, we've decided we're moving the television down here this year. We enjoy being in this room so much more because of the heat, and we've started to hang out here more than we used to. I like having a fire; I like the visual part of it, the sound of kernels dropping into the fire is relaxing. It's therapeutic in a way to sit here and feel warm from the constant heat.

What reactions have you had from family?

Ginger: It's been fun. It's been interesting. Our grandson is a sixth grader and he's really been interested in it and understanding the concept. And that's kind of neat to know that the next generation down will have that awareness of why we're doing this.

Glen: He was talking about global warming one day, because they're really teaching that in school. I told him, "This doesn't really contribute to that, Dillon."

Ginger: And my brother-in-law visited from Detroit last winter and he was just totally baffled by it. He sat down here and just couldn't believe it and thought it was awesome. My sister says he just tells everybody.

Our kids, Josh is 32 and Jay is 26, they weren't sure why we were doing this at first. I thought Josh's comment was funny—one day, he said, "Do you realize you talk about 'corn people' now?" I said, "What do you mean?" We have a houseboat, and he said, "you talk about the 'boat people' and now you talk about 'corn people.'"

What type of people are "corn people"?

Glen: I think that people in that group are mechanical, they're tinkerers, they're experimentalists, alternatives, they're always wanting to talk to the other guy and see how much you got out of yours and if yours is working. You know, they haven't been perfect. There are little glitches, and it seems you get answers more so from people than you do out of the company.

Ginger: That's a part of that group of people, you know. You're able to talk about things, solve things.

Have you had any maintenance trouble with your stove?

Glen: Right now this one isn't working at top efficiency. I don't know how many stoves they've vented out a fireplace. Most corn burners you only have to stick a pipe out the wall a few feet. This one goes 6-8 feet up into the chimney of the fireplace. I can't get it up to setting number 3 or so—it's plenty warm, but when you pay that much for something, you want to see it work. Ed said we need to take those pipes all the way up through the chimney and described why. He found that out because somebody else had done that. It's not something that I think the company could tell you.

Have you had any other surprising experiences with your corn stove?

Glen: There's another group of friends that we haven't told you about, and that is the animals. The corn spills and it keeps them fed in the winter. The squirrel only eats the center out of the kernel and after he's done the kernel is broken, so that makes it easier for the snow birds. Rabbits, I don't think they care one way or the other.

Ginger: It's birds that we've never had before, pheasants, here in town. It's fun to watch them. Here we are in the middle of the city.

Glen: Of course in the spring we're weeding corn out of our garden.

What is the most compelling reason to burn corn in your home?

Glen: I'm the old hippie, in the past. I've always been interested in this stuff, for many, many years, probably since the first issue of *Mother Earth News.*

I don't know if it was so much about the environment at first as it was people telling you that you have to pay so much to heat your house and then giving them your money. I don't like that and there's got to be a better way. I think that was it more than any environmental concerns initially; I've got to do it cheaper. I can't be strapped to any company that can dictate to me how much I pay all the time. There are these that say the sources of natural gas are limited and these that say there's plenty. They can tell you what they want to tell you and control the prices just like we saw with the fuel this summer, and that's kind of scary.

And I think Iowa is poised to really lead the nation and show people biomass or alternative forms of a lot of things. I think a lot of our state government is poised to make that happen. They know there's money in it, and a lot of them are conscious about the environment now, too. It's a whole different generation of people.

Five things alone are necessary to the sustenance and comfort of the dark ones among the children of earth.

"The sun, who is Father of all.

"The earth, who is mother of men.

"The water, who is the Grandfather.

"The fire, who is the Grandmother.

"Our brothers and sisters the Corn, and seeds of growing things."

-Zuni Priest, 1884

Denny Doderer

Location: Rochester, IA
Number of winters with a corn stove: 2

How did you heat your home before the corn stove?

I'm probably one of the few people who heated with exclusively wood. Growing up we heated with a regular old gas powered stove in the basement. In the two years before I moved to California, I rented a house that was heated by LP gas, and it went through an entire tank per month.

What led you to consider heating with corn?

I live in a big airy room, about 1300 square feet, the heat was going right up through the ceiling and heating the upstairs. Because the place is under renovation there tend to be big, gaping holes. The wood burning fireplace insert was not keeping the place warm, or it was keeping it too hot. The fireplace only has a certain range. Bringing wood into the house is dirty and when you're burning it, every time you open the door, dust and ashes come out, and I inevitably smelled like a fireplace.

The corn stove doesn't have a distinct smell. I know people with big houses who manage to keep their whole house warm with one corn stove.

What do you envision for the future of corn stoves?

I say that burning corn is high tech-low tech. It's a lot of low tech in that you're striking a match to something, fuel being augured in, and the fuel has to be delivered to your home by a separate mechanism. The high tech aspect of it is that corn burning stoves are becoming more sophisticated all the time and are beginning to get more features. They're getting better, because it's a new industry.

If you live in a place like Iowa, corn is cheap and I think there's a really good future for it. I think the big changes are going to be made in how the corn is delivered. A current benefit to LP gas and heating oil is that it's delivered in pipes and the whole

infrastructure is in place. People are going to have bigger capacity to store corn at home, because we won't want to use a bunch of gasoline having corn delivered frequently. I just think that whatever we can do to not be dependent on foreign oil and these other unstable economies is worth it. We should not be making bad foreign policy because of our thirst for fossil fuel. This is much deeper than our need for fossil fuel, it affects everything our government does. We're just so utterly dependent on oil, and it just makes no sense.

Do you have reactions from friends?

All of my friends are kind of amused by it. A lot of people thought it was a gimmick, but once they had to start paying natural gas bills, they thought the corn stove was pretty neat.

What challenges have you had with your stove?

This is an older model and there were a couple of times that I couldn't get it to start. The other problem I have, because I don't own a pickup truck, is managing the amount of fuel I have on hand. I would take about three plastic containers in my car and fill them up. I wouldn't burn corn all day long, I would turn it off or down low.

The corn stove will keep the room warm if the temperature is above about 22 degrees, but after that I need to burn wood in my fireplace. People who live in modern houses tend to have a controlled environment, they tend to not have big gaping holes where cold air comes through. Every day I had to make decisions. I couldn't really leave town for a weekend if it was going to be really cold. I can keep the fire going a longer time with the corn stove than the fireplace.

Industry Experts

The following individuals were chosen for their influence on and understanding of the modern biomass fuel industry, to share their assessment of the industry now and where it may be in 5-10 years.

Despite the diversity of particular focus comprised by this group of individuals, there is consensus among them that corn is but a jumping-off point for this burgeoning industry, which will soon widely embrace many other sources of biomass that are well suited as sources of energy. They are in agreement that biomass fuels are best produced with as little energy as possible, sourced locally through efficient delivery systems, and made from waste products whenever possible. They call for continuing innovation of stoves and fuel sources and for government incentives to further develop and to use this renewable energy technology in homes, businesses and industry settings. These are the people at the forefront of the modern biomass industry.

Meet the experts…

W. Allan Cagnoli

Director of Government Affairs
Hearth, Patio & Barbecue Association
Arlington, VA

What is the role of HBPA in the biomass stove industry?

Hearth, Patio & Barbecue Association (HPBA) is an international trade association first established in 1980 to represent and promote the interests of the hearth products industry in North America. The association includes manufacturers, retailers, distributors, manufacturers' representatives, service and installation firms, and other companies and individuals—all having business interests in and related to the hearth, patio, and barbecue products industries.

HPBA's members manufacture, import, distribute, sell, service, and represent products that include factory-built fireplaces, gas logs, inserts, and accessories; wood, pellet, coal, gas and electric stoves; barbecues, grills, smokers and accessories; and, patio furniture and accessories.

Our members make and sell biomass stoves—wood, pellet, corn or other. Our members who do not sell stoves but sell other items, have an interest in the health of what we call the hearth side of the association. Hearth products, whether for recreation or heating, represent a lifestyle, one that often includes outdoor patio living and grilling. So, the interests of our association members are closely tied together, and HPBA looks out for the interests of all our members.

How educated are Americans about alternative biofuel and what perceptions or misconceptions do they have?

The American public has a very good general understanding about biofuel and the benefits of using more biofuel rather than relying on only fossil fuels, from an economic,

the feel-good heat

ecological and national security perspective. However, like the busy consumers we all are, sometimes we can get overwhelmed by the commercial hype about one type of biofuel and miss the larger issue and message. And what is the larger issue? That we need to consider all types of fuels available as having the possibility of becoming a major fuel for the entire nation. I call it "going forward with the past." America has massive biomass resources, enough to fuel much of its energy needs for many centuries. But what is needed is the widespread use of, and continued technical improvements to, biomass fuel products to make its use a national standard, not just a regional preference. HPBA and its members are committed to, and working very hard on, providing our customers with a full line of biomass stove choices, be it wood, pellet, corn, or other, that meet the efficiency and emission needs of today and the future.

Are legislators well informed, and are they committed to advancing the biofuel industry in the United States?

Good products and knowledgeable consumers are not all that is needed. We also must educate our policy makers and regulators about the need to make biomass fuel one of the major components of our Nation's energy plan. And that education is one of HPBA's major goals. Through meetings, seminars, and yes, lobbying by HPBA and our membership, we will be spending the next few years raising the biomass IQ level of as many as we can with the goal of making biomass fuel policy something that works the benefit of all.

What is the biggest hurdle to or misconception about the viability of alternative biofuel and how should that be addressed?

Quite honestly, the lack of an absolute need over the last several decades to use biomass as an energy fuel resulted in a lack of knowledge about it, both from a user and a provider standpoint. Many questions are now being asked, and answered, that were not even considered until recently: What is the best biomass fuel to use in what circumstance; with what heating units; how do efficiency and emissions relate together; what technological advancements will work best, or are needed to be developed; and, what do consumers really want in this era of energy and emissions/global warming awareness?

It is up to HPBA and its members to educate policy makers and the public about the virtues of, and value to the United States and the world, of the virtues of biomass: it is renewable, it is a "carbon neutral" product, it is easily obtained, and it will do the job of providing much of the energy needed in the world. The adoption at the federal, state, and even local level, of public policy statements and policies that support and promote biomass usage is critical. HPBA will be working for the adoption of those policies.

What type of legislation does HBPA advocate to promote the biofuel and biomass stove industries?

HPBA advocates the passage of any legislation that will promote the use of biomass as a heat and energy source fuel. Naturally, an association wants its products used by the consuming world and will push to have them accepted, and we are very confident that our members have the right products to fit the need. But HPBA is looking beyond just the sales aspect of having our products more widely utilized: We know that there will come a time in the not too distant future when energy and emissions issues will create a critical and dangerous period for the world and its inhabitants, and we believe our association has the product and knowledge to help us possibly avoid that moment.

In recent efforts to educate members of the 109th United States Congress (2006-07), HPBA has been successful in getting considered, introduced, and in one case passed, legislative concepts related to the use of biomass and our industry.

The two most successful items were the introduction of a measure (H.R. 3928) to provide a $500 tax credit to consumers who replace pre-1992 wood stoves with new, EPA-certified wood stoves and fireplace inserts. Introduced by Representatives Tim Murphy (PA) and Melissa Hart (PA) and called "The Wood Stove Replacement Act of 2005", this measure was strongly supported by HPBA, but unfortunately did not become law.

Another measure, the "Renewable Energy Security Act of 2005" did become law as part of the Energy Policy Act of 2005, the first comprehensive federal energy policy to pass Congress since 1992. RESA, as it is called, provides a discount of 25%, up to $3000, for consumers who choose renewable energy appliances, including pellet stoves, with a thermal efficiency rating of 75%. While this language is now part of federal law, the money to fund the discount (provided as a rebate from the Dept. of Energy) has not been provided in accompanying appropriations bills, so RESA, while good policy, remains somewhat toothless without the money.

In addition to supporting other measures which will help in the promotion and use of biomass fuel in the United States, HPBA will be working with the new 110th Congress and the Administration to get passed both a new version of Murphy-Hart and the RESA appropriations.

I am able to prove from the sacred writings that wine and corn were used by men before the offspring of Coelus and Saturnus. —Lactantius

Lee Strait

Operations and Financial Manager
Practical Environmental Solutions,
Inc., Washington, IA

What role does Practical Environmental Solutions, Inc., play in the biomass industry?

The mission statement of Practical Environmental Solutions, Inc. is to play a part in the revitalization of the Iowa economy and to help Iowa become energy independent by utilizing Iowa resources to make a clean and renewable form of energy.

Practical Environmental Solutions, Inc. (PES) was started as an S-Corporation in May 2005 by my father, Michael Strait, who is the president of the company and myself, the Operations and Financial Manager. Since the start-up another son of Michael's, Justin Strait, has joined the company as the Head Maintenance Manager.

In Sept. 2006, PES purchased a 27,000 ft² feed mill and warehouse facility located in an industrial park in Washington, IA that had been vacant since May 2003. PES is currently in the process of refurbishing and rerouting the existing equipment setup to make wood pellets for use in residential heating applications. *PES Biomass Power Pellets* will be sold at stove dealerships in the Washington and Iowa City area and other outlets will be sought.

PES Biomass Power Pellets will be made from wood waste produced at Iowa based sawmills and furniture manufacturers. PES currently has an agreement to receive ~16 tons per day of wood shavings and will seek out more sources as production is perfected.

The demand for wood pellets has increased at a huge rate over the last 3 years because of rising heating costs and increased awareness of alternative fuel sources. *PES Biomass Power Pellets* are a renewable and locally produced alternative heat source to electricity, natural gas, propane and heating oil. In 2006, it was projected that for the first time ever biomass fuel stoves (corn and wood pellet) will outsell natural gas stoves.

How is pelleting wood a solution to greater challenges (waste, energy, etc.) we face today?

The greatest motivation behind biomass for energy, especially in a resource-rich state such as Iowa, is that it can be locally produced and utilized. Most coal and natural gas supplies used in Iowa originate from another state. The people of Iowa have realized that they don't have to rely on the big energy companies' natural gas or coal supplies to keep warm. They can use biomass fuel produced locally and, ultimately, improve the economy and environment of their communities.

With that being said, it should be pointed out that pelleting wood is *not* a solution to our nation's energy problems; it is only a small piece of the biomass energy puzzle. This is because manufacturing wood pellets can make economic and environmental sense only if by-products of wood milling and manufacturing are used, making it supply limited. It would be impossible to cut down a forest of oak trees to make wood pellets economically. Wood pellets are the highest end value use of the waste wood shavings and sawdust produced in the furniture and saw milling industries.

In college, I was a Pollution Prevention Intern (P2) with the Iowa Department of Natural Resources. This program focused on reducing pollution and waste from large industry to ultimately reduce their operating expenses. My host company's ambivalence about their environmental impact was erased when I proved to them that they could save over $80,000 per year by implementing several environmentally friendly changes.

The creative and environmentally friendly reduction/reuse of industrial waste will lead to greater resource utilization, an improved economy and a cleaner environment. The growing use of biomass stoves signifies a heightened awareness about resource conservation and renewable energy.

What role can biomass and waste-derived fuels play in the world's energy future?

Waste-derived biomass fuels can provide a significant percentage of our nation's energy needs but will never be able to replace all the coal, natural gas and petroleum needed to satisfy the enormous energy appetites of the American public. Energy conservation needs to become the number one priority before biomass fuels can reach their full potential. By using less energy and/or by using energy that is local, renewable and clean, our country will improve our natural environment and strengthen our local economies to a great degree.

What other forms of waste (biomass or otherwise) are candidates for production of energy and heat?

There are many forms of biomass fuel available to produce energy and heat. The raw material for biomass fuels can come in the form of industrial by-products or green (fresh) feedstock. (Side note: I would like to stop referring to the biomass as 'waste' because it only furthers the idea that it is not valuable; more often than not there is potential for reuse. A new phrase needs to be coined to show the true value of the biomass. Recycled energy? Organic energy?)

Waste is discarded because of inefficient processes and/or ambivalence about the value contained within these resources. When an industry produces waste, they are using resources inefficiently and getting hit in the pocketbook again when paying to dispose of that waste. The economics prove that more efficient use of our resources is the only way to have a truly sustainable society.

There are several other forms of biomass that are being developed or are currently being used as energy sources, including (but certainly not limited to), soy bio-diesel, ethanol, switchgrass, DDG's from ethanol production, corn kernels, corn cobs, corn stover, animal waste and municipal solid waste. Each biomass form presents its own hurdles to convert it to a usable energy source. Some biomass forms have great potential as fuel but have heavy processing burdens. Using biomass for energy requires the innovative use of conversion and handling technologies.

Practical Environmental Solutions, Inc. has set the goal to be a Zero-Waste Industry; all wood that comes in will leave in pellet form or will be utilized on-site in wood pellet stoves.

What type of support is needed to continue the development of biofuel and waste fuel markets?

Our legislature needs to encourage the development of small businesses, such as Practical Environmental Solutions, and set priorities for the development of clean, locally-produced, renewable fuel. These goals will bolster a community's self-reliance and put our resources to the most efficient use. The only way to sustain our world is for people to subsist on the resources surrounding them and cut out unnecessary waste.

Jay Wheeler,

California Cornstoves &
Century Farm Harvest Heat

What is your role in the bio-fuel industry?

In 2000 or 2001 I was in Illinois and found a used book that mentioned corn stoves. It was unusual for anyone on the West Coast to be looking into them, so manufacturers would offer to send me dealer packs. I just put up a very simple web site, and I didn't try to push them hard but people really showed curiosity. I started getting all sorts of letters and questions. I put a nicer web page up and until about a year ago, I was the only person on the West Coast who sold corn stoves. I sold the company about a year and a half ago, and I still love the game. At the moment I am a consultant and spokesperson for California Cornstoves and a consultant and information person for Century Farm Harvest Heat. People still call me just to talk about corn stoves all the time. It's not unusual to get people calling form Canada. When you get down to the nuts and bolts I'm not the best mechanic but I know how different stoves will perform.

What changes have you seen in the biofuel industry during the time you've been involved?

Biomass heating stoves have become a much bigger seller in the last few years. This is due to three reasons:

A. People becoming more ecologically minded. Corn stoves are appealing because of the cleaner emissions, lack of pollution and the fact that biomass is a renewable resource. You can grow a new corn crop in 120 days.

B. More sophisticated stoves. In the past, stoves needed to be shut down and cleaned out daily. Today many are self-cleaning and maintenance doesn't need to be done nearly as often. Several new stoves have igniters in them and can be thermostatically controlled. There are lots of advancements and talk of having a hopper outside of your house where you push a button and it augurs it into your stove or basement. These things are not just dreams anymore, there are people doing them.

C. People searching for less expensive heating.

What advice would you give consumers researching corn and pellet stoves for their home or business?

My advice to a potential customer would be that at the present time they must realize that there is work involved when having a biomass stove. You don't just turn up the thermostat. It needs feeding, cleaning, and maintenance.

Some people are buying them because it's a cheaper fuel source and they don't care about the extra work. People tend to want the fanciest stoves, but sophisticated control panels and computerized parts can add to maintenance, as opposed to an on/off toggle switch.

Does the current agriculture industry have the capacity to meet an increasing biofuel demand and an increasing population to feed?

Agriculture can support biomass stoves now and a long way into the future. At present there is a lot of agricultural waste that has the potential to be used. A lot of experimenting is being done trying new, and faster growing fuels.

In the Midwest they've been experimenting with switchgrass. I was really flabbergasted at the number of biomass stoves in Ireland and the fact that they were making biomass pellets out of willow trees that are growing wild. In Canada they burn a lot of wheat—the seed itself. Here I know that I've played around with burning olive pits. Olive pits burn hotter than corn, ignite more easily and burn longer. A couple of the stoves I've sold are capable of burning cherry pits. Apricot pits, peach pits, all those things can be ground and pelletized.

What improvements would you like to see in the biomass industry?

When I'm in contact with different corn stove companies, I stress two things, noise and size. There are some stove companies that are really trying to make quiet stoves now. I'm known for telling them to keep going smaller and smaller. In California and the southern states, a small stove would be perfect. It's amazing how many people would like to have a small stove for their kitchen. It would be so easy to make a small stove that had a convertible top for cooking as well.

If I were going to start a company right now, it would be a small water boiler that could be used for heating a swimming pool, or for radiant floor heating.

"Measure the corn of others
with your own bushel"
—Yiddish Proverb

Bill Bliss
Bliss Industries, Founder

What is the role of Bliss Industries in the biomass industry?

Bliss Industries supplies 21st century pellet processing equipment such as hammer mills for grinding grains and celluloses, pellet mills and coolers for pelleting wood, corn stover, seed cleanings and ethanol fuel. Bliss Industries continues to advance their equipment to provide improved production and cost to the manufacturer and the consumer.

Describe Bliss Industries history manufacturing Pellet Mills.

Bliss Industries was licensed in 1991 to manufacture and market the Robinson Milling Paladin Pellet Mills in North America. We put our first two pellet mills into operation in late winter of 1992 pelleting swine feeds, and those pellet mills are still operating. We saw an opportunity in the late 90s to get into the cellulose/wood pelleting industries and have many units pelleting woods of all type in North America.

What influenced the decision to manufacture pellet technology?

We saw the opportunity for many improvements—since most of the pellet mills being marketed were designed in the 1950s with little to no improvements, only making the mills larger with the same needs for improvements. Since we are replacing pellet mills of other manufacture, we feel we are accomplishing some of the necessary improvements we set out to make, still making improvements such as reducing the 100 HP per ton to 75 HP per ton of wood pellets, and we have many more improvements to make that take time and research. For pelleting biomass fuels, we saw a challenging product and took it on because we saw the need for a renewable fuel with fewer emissions. We

119

believe the renewable biomass cellulose fuel pellets are the fuel of the future that can be regenerated each year instead of millions of years to reproduce.

How are quality standards for the pellet industry changing?

I see home heating appliance manufacturers going to stoves and boilers that will burn pellets up to 3% ash content. I think BTUs will become more important than the ash content as the new appliances reach the end user.

Since biomass fuel products are grown on the land and are renewable, I see the environment dictating what biomass fuel will be produced in different areas. The pellet mill manufacturers will have their work cut out for them to improve the mills and to produce quality fuel from various types of biomass at a reasonable cost of production.

How does pellet production and consumption in the U.S. compare to the rest of the world?

It is my understanding that the US and Canada consume a lot more pellets for home heating than any other area. However, it is my understanding that Europe is purchasing a lot of pellet fuel from North America at this time and there are several more large pelleting plants either being constructed or in the planning stages at this time in both the US and Canada. They are also erecting more biomass fuel plants as well.

Where do you see the biofuel industry in 10 years?

I see industrial biofuels for heating schools, hospitals, offices, etc., becoming a very important part of fuel for the world. Europeans are already utilizing biomass pellets for industrial fuel and I see North America using more and more as we become less dependant on foreign oil, with decreased emissions a large part of the deciding factor for going to pellet fuel.

I personally believe that in 10 years we will see biomass fuel as the leader in renewable fuels. Why? There are several reasons. The first, being the economy of North America. We have got to support our agriculture with biofuel crops so they can still produce cheap food. Second, each country must become self-sufficient on fuels and less dependent on the Mid East fossil fuels. Third, with biomass is a great improvement to the emissions problem of fossil fuels. Fourth, biomass fuel is much safer than natural gas or propane; it will not blow up or asphyxiate anyone.

In 10 years I see central boiler (pellet) hot water heat becoming the way of the future for heating homes and businesses of all sizes. Hot water heat is the most efficient heat especially when fired with biomass fuel pellets. In 10 years all fossil fuels will be very pricey and we will have to use it with respect to its cost.

The world has not even begun to start duplication of biomass fuel products. These products are all renewable, some every year and some every 10 to 20 years, not millions of years like the fossil fuels. Renewable fuels will be a big asset for the agricultural economy.

In the age of acorns, before the times of Ceres, a single barley-corn had been of more value to mankind than all the diamonds of the mines of India.
—Henry Brooke

Michael Ott

Executive Director, BIOWA

What is BIOWA's role in the biofuel industry?

BIOWA helps grow the bioeconomy by connecting relevant stakeholders in smart projects. BIOWA connects member's needs and capabilities with opportunities. Investors and target companies are coupled for mutual benefit. We will work with vendors, distributors, scientists, educators, bankers and investors to expand existing businesses and create new sustainable opportunities in regional biorefineries. Biorefineries make ethanol from the entire corn plant, not just the kernel.

What key steps will increase the production and use of biofuels in the US?

First is producing large amounts of ethanol and biodiesel, enough to make headway and get in the public eye. This is just starting to happen. If we want to make serious amounts of biofuels, such as 20+ billion gallons, we need to bring cellulosic ethanol to reality. Right now it works, but is too expensive. That is rapidly changing.

The corn stove industry is great because it gets people in the mindset that corn can be used as fuel, not just for feed. This is an important distinction.

To what extent can biomass energy address and relieve increasing global competition for energy resources?

Current studies, utilizing conservative estimates, suggest that we could produce enough ethanol to completely replace motor fuel in about 15 years. That depends on production of cellulosic ethanol and acceptance of flex fueled cars, which are likely to happen in the near future. A new industry is being created, starting in the Midwest, not the Middle East.

the feel-good heat

What combination of market forces and government incentives will lead to a smooth, effective transition to clean, renewable energy usage in the US?

Demand for E85 will be crucial in spurring transition. I predict that in the next 50 years, we will transform from an oil-based economy to a hydrogen based economy. Biomass will be the bridge between the two. Oil pollutes, is not renewable, and causes tremendous security problems. Biomass solves all of these issues, but isn't currently produced in large enough volumes. The transition from oil to biomass will go through E85. Right now it's a chicken and egg problem, in that there aren't enough flex fuel cars to fill up at E85 stations, and not enough E85 stations to warrant the production of flex fuel cars. The state of Iowa has stepped in to provide funding for gas stations, which is a very good idea. Once people start to see a much cheaper alternative, they will demand E85 and start buying flex fuel cars.

This will spur the growth of the cellulosic ethanol to tremendous volumes, potentially 80+ billion gallons. Once that infrastructure is established, we can start making hydrogen from the same sources using much of the same equipment. The public will be ready for the transition when the fuel sources are ready and available.

How will the US balance its use of agricultural products for food, fiber and energy?

There is a misconception on food vs. fuel. It's not an either-or proposition; you can have both. The by-product of ethanol processing is dried distiller's grains, which are fed to cattle. That is an example of using the same corn kernel for both fuel and food. Existing corn ethanol plants will continue to produce ethanol for some time, but they will eventually be eclipsed by cellulosic sources that produce ethanol from energy crops such as switchgrass. We will have enough food and enough fuel with smart planning and market forces.

Robert Walker
Bixby Energy Systems, Founder

What is your role in the biomass industry?

Bixby has taken on the challenge of attempting to become a leader in the development of Biomass as a significant energy source. Bixby is attempting to establish itself as the primary developer of viable biomass based energy systems that will make the fuel, make the furnaces that will burn the fuel, and also will deliver the fuel to the end consumer. We are developing the technology to make Engineered Fuel Pellets from biomass. We are developing the energy systems (stoves, furnaces, etc.) to convert the energy from these fuels as efficiently as possible into all forms of energy (heat, electricity, etc.). We have acquired a salt delivery company to use as a base for the development of a national distribution system for engineered fuels directly to the home consumer.

What major improvement have you made to biomass burning? Why has this not been able to be accomplished until now?

We have developed a burn system that has a combustion efficiency of 99.7%. We are the first company to seriously dedicate ourselves to the development of viable high-tech biomass furnace systems. This was largely due to the fact that before Bixby came along, no other company was interested in attempting to harness the potential of biomass. There are 10,000 biomass materials in the U.S. and almost 36,000 throughout the world, each with different characteristics and disciplines. Because of this, the feeling was that biomass, although a large source of energy that grows every year, was so diverse that to harness its potential would require 400 different kinds of pellets to use the various material and 400 different furnaces to burn them.

Bixby solved the problem by creating a "recipe" system which categorized these materials into 4 distinct types based on their characteristics and then figured out how to mix these categories together to create an engineered fuel pellet that would burn the same, regardless of what materials we were using. This was important because it meant that since we could now create a pellet that would burn the same regardless of what made it up, that we could now focus on developing a single furnace that could burn these engineered fuel pellets in a manner that would extract the maximum amount of energy from them.

Which biomass sources make the most sense for use in providing heat?

Actually, the Bixby method of utilizing *all* types of biomass materials means that no particular source needs to be the recommended source. Obviously, very light material will not be practical because if it has to be transported to a pelletizing facility, the freight will make it cost prohibitive. It would not be wise to focus on only selected biomass sources because demand would drive the price up for these materials and render biofuels impractical. Utilizing as wide a variety of these materials as possible will provide for a more stable price and a more promising future for biomass as an energy source.

What sort of delivery system or infrastructure will be most efficient as waste-derived fuels become ubiquitous?

Bixby has already designed a system which allows for the pick-up of biomass materials that can be purchased and delivered economically to a processing facility; made into engineered fuel pellets to standardized fuel for the industry, and then delivered directly to consumer's homes using a system similar to the way propane or fuel oil is delivered to consumers today.

What is your vision of the energy industry in ten years?

We will not learn how to conserve energy so demand will continue to increase. Couple that with the world's increasing demand for energy (China and India in particular) and you have a continuing demand for energy worldwide that will require us to continue to find new sources of energy to keep up. Energy will cost more in the future and that will fund the ability to find new, more expensive means of harvesting energy. As prices go up, economically impractical energy sources will become practical. That is our future.

What type of support is needed to continue the development of biofuel and waste fuel?

The government will have to get involved. Today, incredibly, it still subsidizes oil. It is subsidizing ethanol, wind, solar, and a host of other energy sources. The best thing that it could do is drop all these subsidies so that it would create a level playing field for all types of energy and then provide development funds for new breakthrough technologies that could revolutionize non-fossil fuel sources where we will get our new energy from in the future.

Jim Crutcher

Sales Rep
Harman Stove Company
Elizabethtown, KY

Briefly describe the history of Harman Stove Company.

The Harman Stove Company was incorporated as a business in 1979. Dane Harman built a stove in his basement to heat his home after the high energy costs of the 1970s hit home. Someone saw this stove and asked him to build them one, another person asked, and that is how he started to build stoves. He worked from his basement for a couple years before moving into his garage.

When did Harman begin manufacturing pellet and corn stoves? What factors make biomass worth investment?

Harman Stove Co. built its first automatic stove in the late 1980s. This first auto stove was a coal stoker. They then went into pellet stoves and an official corn stove around 2000. The American people have a lifestyle today that does not leave them with enough time at home to make burning wood successful. The pellet stoves, with their automatic operation, achieve the same result. The consumer is not dependent on foreign oil, they have a low maintenance stove operation, and they can leave the stove unattended for long periods of time.

How have pellet and corn stoves improved and what improvements do you expect to see in the future?

The biggest improvements that The Harman Stove Co. has made are in the control board. This control senses the room temperature and modulates the output of the stove accordingly. This is not an on-off type operation. This is like cruise control on your car, where if you set the speed to 55, the motor does what it needs to do to make your car go 55. The stove works the same way: set the temperature at 70 degrees and the stove produces enough heat to make the home 70. There have been vast improvements in noise reduction, easier access to critical parts for cleaning, and products that are much more user friendly.

I believe that we will see many improvements to biomass stoves in the future. We will see bulk delivery of the fuel to the home and bulk delivery of the fuel to the stove, which will let the consumer go for months without touching the product. I hope that someday we will be burning actual garbage (which we have lots of) and less of the traditional wood based fuels.

Where do you envision the biomass stove industry in the future?

Since 1998 pellet stoves have been the number one category in terms of percentage sold. The biomass industry is at a crossroads in my opinion. The fuel supply has not been able to match the production of stoves. This has left some dealers with an inability to purchase as much fuel as they needed. This has also made prices go up. Corn is readily available, but unless the consumer can handle it in bulk, and buy from the farmer, it is hard to justify the cost of the stove. We need more pellets. We also need a consistent corn that is readily available to anyone that wants to deal with corn as a fuel. Today corn varies so widely from one county to the next, there is no consistency in what will burn well in a particular stove.

We need big buck companies involved in the research and development of corn and corn stoves. Most of the companies involved right now are what you would call small, independent manufacturers. They have no engineering staff, no labs, and are operating by trial and error. They will eventually get it right, but it will take a long time. A large company could easily throw lots of money into developing corn and biomass stoves and have a much better stove in six months than is available now, after 5-10 years of development.

How likely is biomass to become a major source of renewable heat and power in the US?

I cannot envision biomass to be a major source of heat in the US until we see utility prices like the Europeans and many other countries are experiencing today. In our cheap energy market, it is easier to just turn up the thermostat.

All improvements in biomass energy will require that a young generation heeds the warnings of our energy situation and take an interest in research and development. Such is the case of Kirsten Riemann who was awarded the BioEconomy Award in 2006 at the Johnson County, Iowa Fair. Currently a student at Illinois Institute of Technology, Kirsten stressed, upon winning, that she is, "very interested in going into bioprocessing technology. It captivates my attention and I would like to bring about change in the energy market."

Don Kaiser

Executive Director
Pellet Fuels Institute
Arlington, VA

What role does the Pellet Fuels Institute play in the biofuel industry?

The Pellet Fuels Institute is a non-profit association that serves the pellet industry, which is comprised of pellet mills, pellet appliance manufacturers and industry suppliers. The Institute is active in educating consumers about the convenience and practicality of using wood pellet fuel in both residential and commercial applications.

Which sectors are the largest consumers of pellet fuel technology?

It is estimated that there are close to 1 million pellet stoves in use today in North America. The largest consumers in the U.S. are by far residential, with some commercial and industrial usage. Throughout the world, residential usage of pellet fuel is slightly more prevalent than commercial and industrial usage.

How does pellet production and consumption in the US compare to the rest of the world?

Pellet usage in the U.S. ranks fourth behind Sweden, Belgium, and Holland. World pellet usage is estimated at 7 million tons. In North America, pellet producers have historically been able to meet demand for fuel.

Where do you see the pellet industry in 10 years?

In ten years, I believe that pellet usage will continue to increase and that commercial and industrial applications will grow in the United States.

the feel-good heat

What steps is PFI taking to propel biofuel pellets into the mainstream?

PFI aggressively promotes the benefits of using pellet fuel through promotions campaigns, education, and additional outreach efforts. We are also working with local, state, and federal legislative and regulatory bodies to educate them on the benefits of pellet heat.

What effect can pellet fuels have on the American economy?

Pellet fuels can have a significant impact on the American economy. The use pellet fuel enhances our independence from imported oil while providing jobs to local economies. In addition, pellets are safe, clean burning and easy to transport.

Richard Fox, Parks and Recreation Director with the City of Marion, Iowa, on using a corn burning stove at their building: "This is our first experience with the corn burner and we constantly share the positives with the many people who visit the Arts and Environment Center. It is a perfect fit for what we are trying to promote in Marion.

Not only is the stove easy to start and maintain, but it provides plenty of heat from such a small unit. One bucket of corn burns the entire time the staff is working at the center. Weekly maintenance consists of emptying the ashes and cleaning the glass. Start up time is less than 30 seconds which was a real surprise to me. We constantly get comments on the stove as people find it hard to believe that it not only burns corn but that it puts out so much heat. If I hadn't just put in a 'gas' fireplace in my basement two years ago, I would have invested in a corn burning stove myself. I love the idea of using a renewable source to heat plus the `popcorn' smell is pleasant as well."

John Wagor

Vice President Sales and Marketing
St. Croix Pellet and Corn Stoves

What is your background in the energy and biomass industry?

I have been in the combustion engineering and sales industry with Johnson Gas Appliance Co. for 28 years. It is a combustion engineering and manufacturing company that was established in 1901. I have been involved with gas, oil, wood and biomass divisions.

What would you consider the single biggest improvement to the heating industry in the last 30 years?

Increased efficiencies and availability of alternative heating appliances.

Compare and contrast burning gas and biomass for heat.

Natural gas and LP technologies have matured to the point that they, as well as electricity, are the easiest for homeowners to operate. There are little or no concerns about running out of fuel—especially on extended periods away from the home.

Biomass heating technologies have certainly come a long way towards more automatic operation, but they still demand homeowner intervention in the process. I look for continued improvement which will allow more extended, automatic operation in the future.

The homeowner's involvement (e.g. physically loading the hopper, and obtaining the fuel) can also be the attraction to biomass. The individual feels like he or she is now a physical part of the heating process—not simply a revenue source who forks out the cash at the end of the month to "big oil." Being an integral part of the process and truly making a difference is important.

the feel-good heat

The renewable fuel source and independence from foreign oil mystiques are also strong attractions to many.

What trends characterize the current biomass energy industry?

Until biomass technology matures to produce more automatic operation, and fuel supplies are easy to obtain and more reliable, the industry trends will continue to be cyclical. It is too easy to drop back to using oil and gas fuels, when market prices make them attractive. Given equal fuel rates per BTU, the fuel which is more available and easier to use will win out. Biomass must be cheaper than fossil fuels to continue its growth with present technology.

What potential do you see for the widespread use of biomass as a heating fuel?

I feel that we will see steady growth on the average, but no single fuel source will be the panacea for everyone. I foresee niche markets which are dependent on local fuel availability, such as corn, wheat, rye, wood by-products, etc.

What future innovations would you like to see in either biomass stoves or biomass fuels?

As more waste and by-products become available, I imagine that more multi-fuel technology will develop.

Innovation is driven by demand. As more homeowners use and request alternative-fueled appliances, creativity in storage and handling will follow.

I see residential storage units—both above and below ground—with automatic feed systems. These could be filled by local cooperative elevators or entrepreneurial farmers. Supply of bagged biomass fuels will become more available.

Ed Williams, Owner

Century Farm Harvest Heat
www.harvest-heat.com
Iowa City, IA

Describe why you're a promoter of biomass for heating homes.

I see biomass as a whole new transformation into an economy that, if we do it right, can benefit the state, the nation and the world. I see it as the perfect triple bottom line economy, where environmental, societal and economic considerations can all be blended into one. It's the beginning of a whole new industry and it's fun to be part of an emerging industry that most people don't notice.

I imagine that there are 80% of the people in this country who have never heard of a biomass stove, yet the people who have this product just think it's the greatest thing in the world. Five years ago, when I bought my first corn stove, I thought "Eureka! This is a great idea." At that time, I made the comment that in 10 years this stove will be an antique. In reality it took only three years. Now there will be stove technology out in the next three years that will revolutionize the biomass industry for the home.

For customers, the return on investment is huge. There's no other renewable energy source that you can purchase, be it a regenerative hybrid car, a windmill, a solar panel, geothermal—which everyone is anxious to have—that gives you the return on investment that this product does. There is no other appliance that you can buy for your house that is going to pay for itself like this one. It's so logical.

What changes have you seen in biomass stove technology?

The changes I've seen at the hearth expos I've been to in the last few years have been really amazing. In five years we've gone through a manually operated stove with dials that took 15 minutes to light, and which wasn't all that efficient. Now I have a pellet

the feel-good heat

stove on hand with a control board on it looks like an iPod. It has 3 buttons and a digital read out. You can set it and program it just like a thermostat on the wall. So the technology is really improving. The consumer-friendliness is improving. I heard a president of a major stove company say that he wanted to make the first "refrigerator-stove," meaning that when you bring it home, you take it out of the box, plug it in and 10 years later it's still running with very little service.

From an agricultural perspective, why is utilizing biomass for heat and energy an exciting prospect?

If we in agriculture get involved in the processing, adding value to what we grow, that's an opportunity as well. We need to own the biomass processing facilities. There's a whole new pelletizing industry starting in Iowa. We used to have to have product shipped from Canada or Wisconsin or Missouri, and now there are local pellet producers. One company's going to be pelletizing corncobs for the first time, and they're excited about doing it. The Midwest and Iowa are really just beginning in this whole transformation of the bioeconomy, that George Washington Carver foresaw a hundred years ago. And there are so many more people around the globe who understand this more than we Iowans do. Sometimes we miss what's right in front of us.

How do you respond to the arguments that the process of producing corn is not environmentally friendly or that we should not burn food for heat?

Growing corn can be an extreme process, but in my time we've gone from using the plow to no-till, where we leave the residue on the surface, we used to put on gallons of herbicide or chemicals per acre, now we use ounces per acre and it's far less hazardous and more environmentally benign chemicals. Everything we use now basically has to be degradable, and break down into basic components within a short period of time.

We're getting better. I've read that agriculture has reduced energy usage by 30% in the last 20 years by no-till and reduced use of inputs. I've seen it in my farming career

—much less energy used, not only in fuel but in also in products. And the article said that if the rest of America had reduced their energy usage by the same, we would be in much better shape.

In agriculture, we adopt efficiency because it makes financial sense; we're growing crops which normally provide a low return per acre compared to other high-value crops. The value of corn today in inflation-adjusted dollars is less today than it was during the depression. We're growing a commodity, a commodity that over the long term is $2 a bushel, with increasing overhead costs to grow it.

More and more, people are not hungry because of lack of food, people are hungry because of distribution problems, political situations, wars, whatever. We're growing feed corn, that's used for ethanol, feed for livestock. I was at a conference and saw the Union of Concerned Scientists and Environmental Defense there, all supporting biofuels with corn, because that's the infrastructure we have and it's only a starting point, a jumping off point. In five years it will be other crops. Corn for stoves is normally feed for livestock, not for human consumption. It's a shame this corn has more economic value when used as calories for heat than calories for food.

What if the price of corn goes up?

My first comment is that it's probably not going to last long term. I've followed the price of corn for 30 years and it has stayed at $2 bushel. But if it does stay up higher long term for use in energy products like ethanol, it means that all the other energy sources are also going up. We're not going to get married to a specific biomass source, be it corn or any other source of biomass.

What other forms of biomass do you see being used in the future and where do you see the biomass industry in 10 years.

Of course the holy grail of biomass is switchgrass. Europe does a lot with a perennial grass called miscanthus. They're experimenting with it now here in the US. It can produce three times the biomass per acre as switchgrass, the first year even. So it's a much more rapidly growing perennial grass.

In ten years I see having distributed energy being available with biomass facilities generating electricity for the home. We'll have regional biomass power generating facilities that will distribute heat and power to multiple homes. Maybe not in 10 years, who knows the time frame? The whole biorefinery process makes so much sense from a security standpoint. When you look at what happened when the hurricanes went through the gulf, and hit those two refineries, it really affected our whole energy infrastructure. So, whether it's natural environmental issues, natural disasters, or terrorism issues, to have a regional energy system makes so much more sense.

What kind of support is needed to get to the point where we have regional biorefineries and neighborhood biomass heating systems?

If you look towards Europe, we're not doing anything new here in America. Biomass and biofuels and wood chip usage in Scandinavian countries has been 10x greater. So we need to look around us and see what's possible. In part the energy costs are going to be what drives it. It also seems like it's going to take a grass roots effort to get any sort of political support.

Three years ago I went to a bioconference where the US Department of Defense had a booth, and I stopped and picked up some of their information. They see the future—they don't want to rely on petroleum to fight the next war, or to send the next ships out. If we've got the Department of Defense putting research money into biomass and bioenergy and they see a need for it, it's going to happen.

Five years ago I started touting this corn stove and the whole bioeconomy concept and 98-99% of the people I talked to said, "well that's cool." I've never encountered any other agenda, any other ideology, any other concept where you could get even 70% support because someone's always going to complain. Because it seemed to be environmentally smart, economically smart, politically smart, it was a no brainer. And the number of times I've heard people say "gee, you'd think...." Gee you'd think the legislature would give a tax credit, gee you'd think that every farmer would have one… I've heard a lot of gee, you'd thinks, and now we're starting to think.

What aspect of the stoves or fuel would you innovate or redesign?

We need to design a system that brings the fuel into the home, if not directly into the stove, using an auger system or air system and an outside storage bin that will be filled by delivery people. People are coming up with their own methods right now for delivering the fuel right into the furnace. We have a customer with a gravity wagon that sits outside his basement window, with a PVC pipe as a chute right into his furnace. There's a gate on the PVC pipe, so when he opens it he has automatic delivery.

How can consumers find a source of grain?

Make friends with a farmer, or a legislator. Certain states are even offering incentives. For example Maryland has a state sales tax exemption for corn stoves, which passed unanimously in both houses of the legislature, because of a passionate group of people who all bought corn stoves. Tacoma Park, MD, a suburb of Washington DC, allowed them to put up a silo on city property, so they could get a semi load delivered at a time delivered and it's a co-op.

How would you describe the group of people who use corn and pellet stoves?

Our customers are all outside the box. Politically they're left, right and center, but they're all outside the box. They're all pioneers in this endeavor and eventually the box will begin to fill, I believe. They're willing to put forth the effort and spend some time to learn about it, all for the reward. I had customers a few years ago who couldn't tell corn from soybeans and now they've become connoisseurs of corn. They look at the kernel and study it and know what will burn well. They're creative, attentive and involved. I am inspired by my customers every day.

Appendices

The History of Corn:
The plant formerly known as teosinte.

Zea mays (maize, corn), the modern descendant of an ancient grass native to tropical Central America, delivers its family secrets through time and space packaged tightly in a tiny kernel, complete with all the components required to produce another leaf-, tassel- and ear-adorned stalk when environmental conditions allow.

Before domestication, teosinte (*Zea mexicana*), modern maize's most ancient known ancestor, grew several stalks, each with tiny ears offering 5-10 seeds, each wrapped in its own husk. The seeds fell easily from the ear and were protected from digestion when passing through the gut of an animal by a hard seed coat. Early Central Americans likely realized the potential of this plant for food, and began cultivating it, saving and planting seeds from plants with desirable qualities. Thus began a co-evolutionary partnership that created the modern plant we know today as corn and fueled the cultural and architectural achievements of the Aztec, Mayan and Incan societies.

The Maya, for example, were corn cultivators and this important commodity was not only their primary crop, but their religion, philosophy and way of life. In her paper on corn deities, Karen Bassie-Sweet reports that Mayan myths concerning the creation of the earth and its preparation for human habitation revolved around establishing the corn cycle. The Maya believed that the creator deities, like the male corn god figure at right, made the first humans from white corn seed, spit upon by a rain deity, and ground into corn dough from which humans were formed.

By the time Columbus landed in North America, 300 major corn varieties were being grown by Native American tribes from Canada to Chile. Over time, ears with the most desirable characteristics were saved, planted and inbred for several generations to produce pure strains. Small, deformed ears are common among these strains, until crossed with other pure strains, which produced large cobs with many kernels.

There are many ways that maize and its ancestor plants have been modified, both by natural and human selection. During domestication, characteristics that did not allow easy cultivation of this wild plant were removed. Because teosinte seeds showed variable dormancy, only cobs from the current year's harvest were selected for planting the following year, selecting against dormancy. Rather than individual kernel bracts, plants with tenacious glumens, or shucks, enclosing the entire cob were selected. Easy seed dispersal, called shattering, is common among grains but selected out of maize, in favor of the cob retaining the kernels until removed manually. To domesticate maize, several characteristics of the wild plant had to be removed from it's gene pool, allowing for greater ease of cultivation.

What's going on in there?

Inside this iconic seed of maize, protected from desiccation and disease by the outer pericarp and enveloped in a mass of stored food (the endosperm is 90% starch, 10% protein, oils, minerals, etc.), rests a new corn plant in its embryonic state.

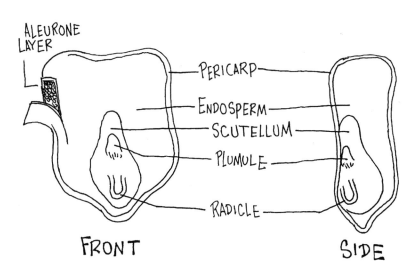

ALEURONE LAYER — PERICARP — ENDOSPERM — SCUTELLUM — PLUMULE — RADICLE

FRONT   SIDE

Hardly more than a minute mass of cells to the naked eye, proto-leaves (called the plumule) and a root-forming radicle are the first definable seedling structures.

Upon reaching 30% moisture, the corn seed slips out of the dormancy phase and into growth. To kick off growth, the sub-pericarp layer known as the aleurone mobilizes the endosperm's energy supply by producing α-amylase, a starch-digesting enzyme. Genetic instructions then choreograph cell growth in the embryo beginning with emergence of the radicle, or root, which, covered by protective sheath known as the coleoptile, anchors the young seedling in the soil. Exposure of the coleoptile to sunlight stimulates elongation of the embryonic leaves and protrusion of the plant shoot. From there, the shoot grows into a leaf- and ear-bearing stalk of about six feet. (To see a corn seed grow from seed to stalk, rapidly flip the pages of this book from front to back and watch the side illustration.)

Types of corn

Dent corn (*Zea mays indentata*) is the principle commercial feed grown in the U.S. and is used in the production of many processed foods. Kernels of dent corn are yellow or white with a soft endosperm that creates a dent as the kernel dries.

Flint corn (*Z. mays indurata*), also known as Indian corn, was named after flint, a very hard stone. Kernels contain little soft starch and do not dent when dried. Ears are long and slender, with eight rows of kernels.

Flour corn (*Z. mays amylacea*), one of the oldest kinds of corn, has a very soft starchy endosperm. It is easily ground and is used in baked goods, but is of limited commercial value in the U.S. Flour and flint corn were the chief types of corn raised by Native Americans.

Sweet corn (*Z. mays saccharata*), due to a single gene preventing conversion of sugar to starch, has more natural sugar than other types of corn. The wrinkled, translucent kernels are eaten on the cob or stored frozen or canned for human consumption.

Pod corn (*Z. mays tunicata*) is not grown commercially, but is raised for scientific research. Each pod corn kernel grows in its own husk, making it difficult to use.

Popcorn (*Z. mays praecox*) has small ears and kernels. Endosperm cells contain an unusually large proportion of water which turns to steam when heated. A hard, dry coat traps the steam and allows pressure buildup until the kernel explodes.

Glossary of Terms

Biomass – Biomass includes all plant matter and plant-derived materials, and often refers to plant materials used as a source of energy.

BTU – British Thermal Unit, a unit of measurement of the energy content of fuels, and also to describe the power of heating systems per hour.

Cellulosic biomass—The leaves and stems of plants, as opposed to the seeds, grains, or nuts. Cellulosic biomass is composed mainly of the sugars cellulose and hemicellulose and the structural polymer, lignin.

Clinker (a.k.a. brick)—Originally used to describe the noncombustible coagulated slag that accumulates when burning coal. The term also applies to noncombustible remains that solidify and collect in the bottom of the firepot of a corn or pellet stove.

Corn stover—The remaining stalks and leaves left over after harvesting the ear of corn. This material may itself be harvested and turned into biomass pellets or processed for ethanol production.

Gravity wagon—Large wheeled corn storage container with an open top and opening at bottom for dispensing corn

UPS—Uninterruptible power supply, or battery backup, maintains a continuous supply of power, which powers devices during momentary power interruptions or when utility power is temporarily unavailable.

Ash and clinker disposal

Corn and pellet combustion produces less ash and clinker residue than burning firewood or coal, and as technology advances, biomass stoves are engineered to produce smaller and smaller volumes of ash and clinker. Proper disposal of clinkers and ash from a biomass stove includes the garden or the compost pile, as this material has no evidence of heavy metals or other contaminants[1], and offers modest fertilization value.

1. Dennis Buffington, "Ash Disposal," 31 October 2005, http://burncorn.cas.psu.edu/disposal.html (5 Sept. 2006).

Stove Accessories, customizing your experience

Every space, from a living room to a garage workspace, has different heating, aesthetic and maintenance needs. Stove accessories allow customization of the stove experience to meet a variety of specific needs. The following is a list of the common stove accessories available today. Some, like hearth pads and storage bins, are necessities for all corn and pellet stove owners. Hopper extensions and extra battery backups are options that add to the convenience of owning a stove, and others like trims and stove finishes add to the appearance of the stove.

Corn cleaner–Corn cleaners sift, and sometimes vacuum out debris like cobs, stalks, leaves, beeswings and dust, allowing the corn stove to produce heat more efficiently.

Storage bin–Storage bins allow storage of several days, weeks, or months worth of corn at a time.

Hopper extensions–Extensions increase the volume of the hopper, allowing it to be filled less often.

Hearth pad – Floor protection from radiant heat is achieved by a ceramic tile hearth pad.

Starter gel – Ignition of some stoves requires this combustible material. Other stoves require a handful of wood pellets, or starter bricks.

Stove color – Most manufacturers offer stoves in a variety of colors and finishes.

Trims – Some models offer choices of colored trims to accent the stove, ie, platnium, gold, etc.

Log sets – Like many gas stove models, some corn and pellet stoves come with a ceramic log set option.

Thermostat kits – Most stoves can be run off a programmable thermostat that will turn the stove on/off when the air reaches a set temperature. Thermostats can be controlled by wall-mounted devices or remote controls.

Various adornments for lids, door faces and handles are available for some stove brands and models.

Biomass Resources featured in this book:

Bixby Energy Systems
www.bixbyenergy.com
14295 James Road
Rogers, MN 55374
877-500-2800

Pellet Fuels Institute
www.pelletheat.org
1901 North Moore Street
Suite 600
Arlington, VA 22209
703-522-6778

BIOWA
www.biowa.us
5 Buena Drive
Iowa City, IA 42245
319-621-8580

Century Farm Harvest Heat
www.harvest-heat.com
2968 Black Diamond Road SW
Iowa City, IA 52240
319-683-HEAT

Harman Stove Company
www.harmanstoves.com
352 Mountain House Road
Halifax, Pennsylvania 17032
717-362-1422

California Corn Stoves
www.californiacornstoves.com
PO Box 77
Hood, CA 95639
916-775-4999

Hearth, Patio & Barbeque Association
www.hpba.org
1901 North Moore Street, Suite 600
Arlington, VA 22209
703-522-0086

St. Croix/Even Temp, Inc.
www.eventempinc.com
Even Temp
P.O. Box 127
Waco, NE 68460

Bliss Industries, Inc.
www.bliss-industries.com
P.O. Box 910
Ponca City, Oklahoma U.S.A. 74602
580-765-7787

Practical Environmental Solutions, Inc.
408 N. 12th Ave.
Washington, IA 52353
1-319-653-2180, pespellets@gmail.com

Reference:
U.S. Department of Energy
Energy Efficiency and Renewable Energy
Biomass Program
http://www1.eere.energy.gov/biomass/

National Renewable Energy Laboratory
Biomass Research
http://www.nrel.gov/biomass/

Find and contact your U.S. Representative
http://www.house.gov/writerep/

Find and contact your U.S. Senator
http://www.senate.gov/

Look up your state environmental agencies
http://www.epa.gov/epahome/state.htm

Sources for "Energy and the environment"

1. The WorldWatch Institute, "Vital Signs 2006-2007," August 2006, <www.worldwatch.org> (accessed August 2, 2006).

2. Ibid.

3. Emanuel, K. 2005. *Increasing destructiveness of tropical cyclones over the past 30 years*. Nature 436: 686-688.

4. Ibid.

5. Global Warming: Early Warning Signs, 1999. <http://www.climatehotmap.org> (accessed October 2, 2006).

6. United Nations, "Millennium Ecosystem Assessment," March 2005, <www.millenniumassessment.org> (accessed September 3, 2006).

7. The WorldWatch Institute, "Vital Signs 2006-2007," August 2006, <www.worldwatch.org> (accessed August 2, 2006).

8. United Nations, "Millennium Ecosystem Assessment," March 2005, <www.millenniumassessment.org> (accessed September 3, 2006).

9. The WorldWatch Institute, "Vital Signs 2006-2007," August 2006, <www.worldwatch.org> (accessed August 2, 2006).

10. International Energy Agency, "Renewables in Global Energy Supply," 2006, www.iea.org (accessed October 3, 2006)

11. National Rewnewable Energy Laboratory, *Learning About Renewable Energy*, August, 12, 2006, < http://www.nrel.gov/learning/> (accessed October 3, 2006)

pg. ♦Mayan Corn God figure Karen Bessie-Sweet, "Corn Deities and the Complementary Male/Female Principle," September 2000, < www.mesoweb.com/features/bassie/corn/media/Corn_Deities.pdf> (September 19, 2006).

Meet The Author and Editor ...

 **Sheila Samuelson** became a friend of Century Farm Harvest Heat in 2004 when she introduced herself to Ed Williams as "a big fan of biomass." With roots in the Midwest and forever an Iowa Hawkeye at heart (her father "Sharm" was named after an Iowa Hawkeye basketball coach), Sheila followed her passion for sustainability issues to San Francisco in fall of 2006. There, Sheila is working towards a "sustainable MBA" from the Presidio School of Management in San Francisco, which she will use to help guide businesses and organizations toward more sustainable business models.

 **And the artist** ... Joe Sharpnack is an Iowa based political cartoonist who finds no ethical conflict in profiting from drawing pictures of corn.

Additional Ice Cube Press Books
Of Midwestern Interest

Letters To A Young Iowan: Good Sense From the Good Folks of Iowa for Young People Everywhere
1-888160-21-7, $19.95, Zachary Michael Jack
What's the single most important piece of advice you would share with a young Iowan growing up or coming of age in the Hawkeye State? Iowa editor and author Zachary Michael Jack posed this timeless question to more than 100 Iowa luminaries, asking them to respond in a letter to all Iowans. The result … a once-in-a-lifetime collection of common sense and hard-won wisdom penned for young people everywhere by a who's who of contemporary Iowans, including the likes of Dan Gable, Robert D. Ray, Mary Swander, and Christie Vilsack.

Firefly in the Night: A Son of the Middle West
1-888160-20-9, $16.95, Patrick Irelan
A candid and humorous story of a life repeatedly interrupted by emergencies. Irelan tells his story the only way he can, with more humor than the events recorded might seem to require. As a child he learned a set of values from his parents and other elders. He has lived his life according to those values, but with occasional revisions that have allowed him to survive the absurdities of modern times.

River East, River West: Iowa's Natural Borders
1-888160-24-1 , $12.95
Writings by David Hamilton, John Price, Gary Holthaus, Lisa Knopp, and Robert Wolf, with "creekography" by Ethan Hirsh, on the meanings, history, folklore, nature and ideas of the two rivers bordering our state. As this book shows, the Mississippi and Missouri Rivers are much more than the water that flows in them.

Prairie Weather
1-888160-17-9, $10
Iowa is at the crossroads of the elements—just above our heads whirl other-worldly tornadoes, and summers bring bone-drying droughts while winter brings walls of snow. In our region of four seasons, we can learn much from our weather. Writing and photographs by Jim Heynen, Mary Swander, Deb Marquart, Amy Kolen, Ron Sandvik, Mark Petrick, Ethan Hirsh, Robert Sayre, Thomas Dean, Patrick Irelan, Michael Harker, Scott Cawelti, and a foreword by Denny Frary.

Living With Topsoil: Tending Our Land
1-888160-99-3, $9.95
A full-fledged exploration via Iowa's finest authors into living with our state's world-famous topsoil. New and valuable writing by Mary Swander, Connie Mutel, Michael Carey, Patrick Irelan, Thomas Dean, Larry Stone and Tim Fay, and an introduction by Steve Semken. Jose Ortega y Gassett once wrote, "Tell me where you live and I'll tell you who you are." You'll find out what it means to live in the land of amazing topsoil once you read this book.

The Good Earth: Three Poets of the Prairie
1-888160-09-8, $9.95
Surprisingly, there is a strong tradition of prairie poetry in Iowa. This work features the prairie-based works of legendary poets Paul Engle, James Hearst and William Stafford. Examined, respectively, by Robert Dana, Denise Low and Scott Cawelti, with a foreword by Iowa farm poet Michael Carey. In the tradition of place-based stories, this book finds connections between spirit and place. As if that isn't amazing enough, this collection also includes one previously unpublished poem by Iowa's famed Writers' Workshop director Paul Engle.

Prairie Roots: Call of the Wild
1-888160-12-8, $10.95
An exploration into the meanings of the wild in the Midwest featuring one of the last published essays of the late Minnesota author, Paul Gruchow. This intriguing collection explores other facets of Iowa and the prairie landscape: a fascinating examination of landscape art by Joni Kinsey, the results of the "grid" system laid upon our land by Robert Sayre, poetry by Mary Swander, the flight and call of geese by Thomas Dean and a discovery of giant worms by Steve Semken. Photography by Rev. Howard Vrankin.

Words of a Prairie Alchemist, Denise Low
(Poet Laureate, State of Kansas)
1-888160-18-7, $11.95
The Great Plains of the North American continent have dramatic seasons, intense colors, alchemical thunderstorms, and epic winters. Denise Low has emerged as one of the most trusted writers of this region. With a balance of drama and finesse, she describes the juncture between the natural world and the human realm of literature.

Ordering Information:
Books can be ordered directly from our web site at
www.icecubepress.com
or by mail (check/money order) by sending to
Ice Cube Press
205 N Front St.
North Liberty, Iowa 52317-9302

(shipping & handling: $1.60 first book, then .25¢ each additional)

the feel-good heat

The Ice Cube Press began publishing in 1993 to focus on
how to best live with the natural world and understand
how people can best live together in the community
they inhabit. Since this time, we've been recognized by a
number of well-known writers, including Gary Snyder,
Gene Logsdon, Wes Jackson, Annie Dillard, Kathleen
Norris, and Barry Lopez. We've published a number of
well-known authors as well, including Mary Swander, Jim
Heynen, Ted Kooser, Stephanie Mills, Bill McKibben,
Carol Bly, Bill Holm and Paul Gruchow. Check out our
books on our web site, with booksellers, or at museum
shops, then discover why we are dedicated to "hearing the
other side."

Ice Cube Press
205 N Front Street
North Liberty, Iowa 52317-9302
p 319/626-2055 f 413/451-0223
steve@icecubepress.com
www.icecubepress.com

as always, a bow to my partners
Fenna Marie & Laura Lee
with allemandes left and right,
may you both burn on!

Century Farm Harvest Heat & Ed Williams are available for consultation, presentations, writing and other learning opportunities related to the present and future bioeconomy. He can tailor specialized experiences for different age groups from grade school through seniors. Learning about and exploring this global transformation is an opportunity for everyone.

FMI: Phone: 319.683.Heat (683.4328)
Email: info@harvest-heat.com

Century Farm Harvest Heat
2968 Black Diamond Rd. SW
Iowa City, Iowa 52240-8454

the feel-good heat